Gai Valeri Catulli
Veronensis Liber

The Poems of
Gaius Valerius Catullus

with an English translation

by

Francis Warre Cornish M.A.

Late Fellow of King's College, Cambridge

Cambridge:
at the University Press

1904

CAMBRIDGE
UNIVERSITY PRESS

University Printing House, Cambridge CB2 8BS, United Kingdom

Cambridge University Press is part of the University of Cambridge.

It furthers the University's mission by disseminating knowledge in the pursuit of education, learning and research at the highest international levels of excellence.

www.cambridge.org
Information on this title: www.cambridge.org/9781107440647

© Cambridge University Press 1904

First published 1904
First paperback edition 2014

A catalogue record for this publication is available from the British Library

ISBN 978-1-107-44064-7 Paperback

PREFACE.

WHEN I began, many years ago, to attempt a translation of Catullus, I had no intention of preparing a text as well. I meant to take the best printed text at hand and adhere to that: but as the work went on, I found myself (a common experience) unable to accept any existing text without modifications. Some editions defer too much to the manuscripts, which are late and bad; others hardly do justice to the work of Italian scholars of the 15th and 16th centuries; and in recent years the authority of Munro, a great but not infallible scholar, has been set too high. So far as I can judge, the best of the current texts is that of Dr Postgate, and I have never departed from it without reluctance.

My principle has been in the main to follow the manuscripts as interpreted by the scholars of the Renaissance, many of whose readings have been universally accepted, and to take account of all modern emendations. Where neither MSS. nor conjectures gave a sufficiently probable reading, I have retained the MS. reading with the sign †. Where a modern emendation seemed to be certain or very probable, I have adopted it with the sign *.

Without going deeply into the question of the MSS. of Catullus, I may briefly say that all[1] are based upon codex Veronensis (V), which 'reappeared at Verona at the beginning of the 14th century and was afterwards lost to the world once more[2].' Two transcripts of this exist; Cod. Sangermanensis (G) at Paris (A.D. 1375)[3], and Cod. Oxoniensis or Canonicianus 30 (O) at Oxford, written about 1400 A.D.[4] The signature V represents the reading of the lost Veronensis as established by G and O. Other MSS. which stand in a near relation to G and O and throw light on V are Cod. Datanus at Berlin (D), 1463, to which a high place is given by Professor Ellis; Cod. Venetus (M) in the Library of St Mark at Venice, a manuscript highly valued by Baehrens; and Cod. Romanus (R), discovered in the Ottoboni collection of the Vatican Library in 1896 by Professor W. E. Hale of the University of Chicago, and collated by him, as well as by Professor Robinson Ellis, but not yet published. By the kindness of Professor Hale and Professor Ellis I have been able to consult the collation of R. It helps to settle cases where G and O do not agree; but the only new reading which I have been able to add to my text is XLIX *7 omniums* for *omnium*. M,

---

[1] Except Cod. Thuaneus (T) of the IXth or early Xth century, which contains Carm. LXII only.

[2] Munro, Introduction, p. iv.

[3] Perhaps not a direct copy of V: see below on Cod. Romanus.

[4] Professor Hale would place the date of O fifty years earlier, and has announced a paper upon its first ownership. The date of the lost MS. which is the parent of G and R he believes to have been 1375, in accordance with the reasoning already given for G by Chatelain in his Paléographie des Classiques Latins, première livraison.

according to Professor Hale, is in the main a copy of R, though the scribe had both R and G before him, and occasionally followed the reading of G; while R is a copy, and, as regards the variant readings, a fuller copy, of the MS., now lost, (X), (itself copied from V) which is the immediate parent of G.

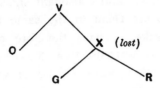

It is impossible to restore with certainty the orthography of Catullus. The MSS. give little help, though they have preserved some of the earlier forms which were current at the time. I have, I believe, printed few if any orthographical forms which Catullus could not have used: but in doubtful cases I have admitted forms justified by the usage of the Augustan age, an age in which much attention was paid to orthography, in preference to those found in inscriptions, the tendency of which is to perpetuate archaic spelling.

It is pretty certain that Catullus and his contemporaries wrote QVOI and QVOIVS, not CVI and CVIVS; QVOM, not QVVM, QVM, or even CVM; SVOM, EQVOS, not SVVM, EQVVS. SVVM is found, though rarely, in inscriptions of c. 70 B.C.[1] The substitution in later Latin of V for O probably denotes a gradual change of pronunciation which was progressing in Catullus's

---

[1] Munro, Lucretius, Introduction, p. 39. Augustus has RIVVS RIVVM and not once UO or VO.

time; and I have thought it lawful, on the ground of convenience, to write SUUM, EQUUS, CUI, CUIUS. U and V do not belong to the same alphabet, V being epigraphic, and U cursive, and therefore do not properly denote the distinction between vowel and consonant. But as they have been conventionally accepted for vowel and consonant signs, it may be permissible to use them in the same alphabet for convenience' sake. I have therefore printed such combinations as VULTUS, UVA, NOVUM, instead of UULTUS, VVLTVS or VOLTVS, UUA or VVA, NOVOM.

The same rule of vowel and consonant should strictly apply to I and J, and I can only defend the exclusion of J by the argument that J was unknown to the ancients.

The MSS. of Catullus and inscriptions of his age frequently, but not universally, have EI where later authors wrote I; QVEI FVREI LEIBEREI for QVI FVRI LIBERI. I have given I in all cases.

In compound words such as ATTRIBUTUS (ADT.), I have in most cases preferred assimilation as being phonetic, whereas the etymologically correct forms (ADTRIBUTUS, &c.), favoured by grammarians, are for the most part of later date.

The terminations -IS, -EIS, -ES were all in use for accusative plural: and no rigid rule can be drawn. I have followed generally Brambach's[1] rules, bearing also in mind Munro's remarks on this heading

---

[1] Die Neugestaltung der Lateinischen Orthographie, von Wilhelm Brambach, Leipzig 1868; and (by the same author) Hilfsbüchlein für Lateinische Rechtschreibung, translated into English by W. Gordon McCabe, A.M., New York 1877.

(Lucretius, Introduction to Notes I. p. 37), which discourage accurate classification.

The object in view is either to reproduce as far as is possible the original spelling of the poet's time, or to work towards a conventional orthography, to take the place of the convention which was established by the scholars of the revival of letters instead of the mediaeval convention, and maintained its ground almost to our own time. I have adopted the latter alternative, as I should accept the conventional orthography of to-day if I were editing the text of an Elizabethan or Caroline author. And I see no reason why a license which is taken by modern editors in the case of Caesar and Cicero may not on the same ground be used in the case of Catullus.

After all,

accurrere scribas
d ne an *c*, non est quod quaeras atque labores.

It is not easy for an editor to apportion the amount of obligation due to the many scholars on whose work he has constructed his own : but I cannot pass over without a grateful reference the names of H. A. J. Munro, Professor Robinson Ellis, Dr Postgate, Aemilius Baehrens and his editor, K. P. Schulze. My best thanks are due to my friends Mr F. H. Rawlins, Mr H. V. Macnaghten, and Mr A. B. Ramsay for much valuable help, and for the great trouble they have taken in looking through the proof sheets.

F. W. C.

THE CLOISTERS,
    ETON COLLEGE,
        December, 1903.

PRINCIPAL MANUSCRIPTS OF CATULLUS.

V. Codex Veronensis, from which all others (except **T**) are derived ; no longer extant.

G. Codex Sangermanensis or Parisiensis, in the National Library, Paris.

O. Codex Oxoniensis, in the Bodleian Library.

D. Codex Datanus, at Berlin.

M. Codex Venetus, in the Library of St Mark at Venice.

R. Codex Romanus, discovered among the Ottoboni MSS. in the Vatican Library by Prof. Hale of Chicago.

T. Codex Thuaneus, in the National Library, Paris ; contains only Carm. LXII.

EDITIONS REFERRED TO IN THE NOTES.

M. H. A. J. Munro. Criticisms and Elucidations of Catullus. Cambridge 1870.

E. R. Ellis. Text and Commentary. Oxford 1867—1889.

P. J. P. Postgate. Gai Valeri Catulli Carmina. London 1889.

B. Æmil. Baehrens. Catulli Veronensis Liber, nova Editio a K. P. Schulze curata. Leipzig 1883.

M. R. Macnaghten and Ramsay. Poems of Catullus. London 1899.

Hpt. Haupt.

Lach. Lachmann.

Lamb. Lambinus.

Avant. Avantius.

Scal. Scaliger.

Bentl. Bentley.

Heins. Heinsius.

Ital. Early Italian editions.

EXPLANATION OF SIGNS.

†   Reading of codd. corrupt or doubtful.

*   Conjectural emendations admitted into the text.

[   ]   Conjectural additions.

* * *   Lacunae in codd.

. . . or blanks   Passages omitted.

GAI VALERI CATULLI
VERONENSIS LIBER

I

Cui dono lepidum novum libellum
arido modo pumice expolitum ?
Corneli, tibi : namque tu solebas
meas esse aliquid putare nugas,
iam tum cum ausus es unus Italorum   5
omne aevum tribus explicare chartis
doctis, Iuppiter, et laboriosis.
quare habe tibi quicquid hoc libelli,
qualecumque ; quod, o patrona virgo,
plus uno maneat perenne saeclo.   10

II

Passer, deliciae meae puellae,
quicum ludere, quem in sinu tenere,
cui primum digitum dare appetenti
et acris solet incitare morsus,
cum desiderio meo nitenti   5
carum nescio quid libet iocari,
credo ut, cum gravis acquiescet ardor,
sit solaciolum sui doloris,
tecum ludere sicut ipsa possem
et tristis animi levare curas!   10

II a

*   *   *   *

tam gratumst mihi quam ferunt puellae
pernici aureolum fuisse malum,
quod zonam soluit diu ligatam.

I

To whom am I to present my pretty new book, freshly smoothed off with dry pumice stone? To you, Cornelius: for you used to think that my trifles were worth something, long ago when you took courage, you alone of Italians, to set forth the whole history 5 of the world in three volumes, learned volumes, by Jupiter, and laboriously wrought. So take and keep for your own this little book, such as it is, and whatever it is worth; and may it, O Virgin my patroness, live and last for more than one century.   10

II

Sparrow, my lady's pet, with whom she often plays and holds you in her bosom, or gives you her finger-tip to peck and teases you to bite sharply, whenever she, the bright-shining lady of my love, has 5 a fancy for some dear dainty toying, that (as I think) when the sharper pangs of love abate, she may find some small solace of her pain—ah, might I but play with you as she herself does, and lighten the gloomy 10 cares of my heart!

II a (a fragment)

*   *   *   *

This is as grateful to me as to the swift maiden was (they say) the golden apple, which loosed her girdle too long tied.

III

Lugete, o Veneres Cupidinesque,
et quantumst hominum venustiorum.
passer mortuus est meae puellae,
passer, deliciae meae puellae,
quem plus illa oculis suis amabat:　　5
nam mellitus erat suamque norat
ipsam tam bene quam puella matrem;
nec sese a gremio illius movebat,
sed circumsiliens modo huc modo illuc
ad solam dominam usque pipiabat.　　10
qui nunc it per iter tenebricosum
illuc, unde negant redire quemquam.
at vobis male sit, malae tenebrae
Orci, quae omnia bella devoratis:
tam bellum mihi passerem abstulistis.　　15
vae factum male! vae miselle passer!
tua nunc opera meae puellae
flendo turgiduli rubent ocelli.

IV

Phasellus ille quem videtis, hospites,
ait fuisse navium celerrimus,
neque ullius natantis impetum trabis
nequisse praeter ire, sive palmulis
opus foret volare sive linteo.　　5
et hoc negat minacis Hadriatici
negare litus, insulasve Cycladas
Rhodumque nobilem horridamque Thraciam
Propontida, trucemve Ponticum sinum,
ubi iste post phasellus antea fuit　　10
comata silva: nam Cytorio in iugo
loquente saepe sibilum edidit coma.
Amastri Pontica et Cytore buxifer,

III

Mourn, ye Graces and Loves, and all you whom
the Graces love. My lady's sparrow is dead, the
sparrow my lady's pet, whom she loved more than 5
her own eyes; for honey-sweet he was, and knew his
mistress as well as a girl knows her very mother.
Nor would he stir from her bosom, but hopping now
here, now there, still chirped to his mistress alone. 10
Now he goes along the dark road, thither whence
they say no one returns. But curse upon you, cursed
shades of Orcus, which devour all pretty things!
such a pretty sparrow have you taken away from 15
me. Ah, how sad! Ah, poor little bird! All because of you my lady's darling eyes are heavy
and red with weeping.

IV

The galley you see, my friends, says that she was
once the fleetest of ships, and that there was never
any timber afloat whose speed she was not able to
pass, whether she would fly with oar-blades or with 5
canvas. And this (says she) the shore of the
blustering Adriatic does not deny, nor the Cyclad
islands and famous Rhodes and the wild Thracian
Propontis, nor the gloomy gulf of Pontus, where she
who has since been a galley was formerly a leafy 10
forest: for in the height of Cytorus she often rustled
with talking leaves. Pontic Amastris and Cytorus

tibi haec fuisse et esse cognitissima
ait phasellus; ultima ex origine   15
tuo stetisse dicit in cacumine,
tuo imbuisse palmulas in aequore,
et inde tot per impotentia freta
erum tulisse, laeva sive dextera
vocaret aura, sive utrumque Iuppiter   20
simul secundus incidisset in pedem;
neque ulla vota litoralibus deis
sibi esse facta, cum veniret a mari
novissimo hunc ad usque limpidum lacum.
sed haec prius fuere: nunc recondita   25
senet quiete seque dedicat tibi,
gemelle Castor et gemelle Castoris.

V

Vivamus, mea Lesbia, atque amemus,
rumoresque senum severiorum
omnes unius aestimemus assis.
soles occidere et redire possunt:
nobis cum semel occidit brevis lux,   5
nox est perpetua una dormienda.
da mi basia mille, deinde centum,
dein mille altera, dein secunda centum,
deinde usque altera mille, deinde centum.
dein, cum milia multa fecerimus,   10
conturbabimus illa, ne sciamus,
aut nequis malus invidere possit,
cum tantum sciat esse basiorum.

VI

Flavi, delicias tuas Catullo,
ni sint illepidae atque inelegantes,
velles dicere, nec tacere posses.

green with box, my galley says that all this was and
is well known to thee; she says that from her earliest 15
birthtime she stood on thy top, in thy waters first
dipped her blades, and thence over so many riotous
seas brought her owner, whether the breeze from left
or right invited, or Jove came down astern on both 20
sheets at once; and that no vows to the gods of the
shore were made by her all the time she was sailing
from the furthest sea even to this limpid lake.

But these things are past and gone; now she 25
rests in old age and retired leisure, and dedicates
herself to thee, twin Castor, and thee, Castor's twin.

V

Let us live, my Lesbia, and love, and value at
one farthing all the talk of crabbed old men.

Suns may set and rise again. For us, when the
short light has once set, remains to be slept the sleep 5
of one unbroken night.

Give me a thousand kisses, then a hundred, then
another thousand, then a second hundred, then yet
another thousand, then a hundred. Then, when we 10
have made up many thousands, we will confuse our
counting, that we may not know the reckoning, nor
any malicious person blight them with evil eye, when
he knows that our kisses are so many.

VI

Flavius, if it were not that your mistress is rustic
and unrefined, you would want to speak of her to
your Catullus; you would not be able to help it. But

verum nescio quid febriculosi
scorti diligis: hoc pudet fateri.   5

quare quicquid habes boni malique,
dic nobis.   volo te ac tuos amores
ad caelum lepido vocare versu.

VII

Quaeris, quot mihi basiationes
tuae, Lesbia, sint satis superque.
quam magnus numerus Libyssae harenae
lasarpiciferis iacet Cyrenis,
oraclum Iovis inter aestuosi   5
et Batti veteris sacrum sepulcrum,
aut quam sidera multa, cum tacet nox,
furtivos hominum vident amores,
tam te basia multa basiare
vesano satis et super Catullost,   10
quae nec pernumerare curiosi
possint nec mala fascinare lingua.

VIII

Miser Catulle, desinas ineptire,
et quod vides perisse perditum ducas.
fulsere quondam candidi tibi soles,
cum ventitabas quo puella ducebat
amata nobis quantum amabitur nulla.   5
ibi illa multa tum iocosa fiebant,
quae tu volebas nec puella nolebat.
fulsere vere candidi tibi soles.
nunc iam illa non vult: tu quoque, impotens, noli,
nec quae fugit sectare, nec miser vive,   10
sed obstinata mente perfer, obdura.
vale, puella.   iam Catullus obdurat,

(I am sure) you are in love with some unhealthy-looking wench; and you are ashamed to confess it. 5

Well then, whatever you have to tell, good or bad, let me know it. I wish to call you and your love to the skies by the power of my merry verse.

VII

You ask how many kissings of you, Lesbia, are enough for me and more than enough. As great as is the number of the Libyan sand that lies on silphium-bearing Cyrene, between the oracle of sultry 5 Jove and the sacred tomb of old Battus; or as many as are the stars, when night is silent, that see the stolen loves of men,—to kiss you with so many kisses, Lesbia, is enough and more than enough for your 10 mad Catullus; kisses, which neither curious eyes may be able to count up nor an evil tongue to bewitch.

VIII

Poor Catullus, 'tis time you should cease your folly, and account as lost what you see is lost. Once the days shone bright on you, when you used to go so often where the maiden led, the maiden loved by me as none will ever be loved. There were 5 given us then those joys, so many, so merry, which you desired nor did the maiden not desire. Bright to you, truly, shone the days. Now she desires no more—no more should you desire, poor fool, nor follow her who flies, nor live in misery, but with re- 10 solved mind endure, be firm. Farewell, maiden; now Catullus is firm; he will not seek you nor ask you

nec te requiret nec rogabit invitam:
at tu dolebis, cum rogaberis nulla
scelesta, *nocte.　quae tibi manet vita?　15
quis nunc te adibit? cui videberis bella?
quem nunc amabis? cuius esse diceris?
quem basiabis? cui labella mordebis?
at tu, Catulle, destinatus obdura.

IX

Verani, omnibus e meis amicis
antistans mihi milibus trecentis,
venistine domum ad tuos Penates
fratresque unanimos anumque matrem?
venisti.　o mihi nuntii beati!　　　5
visam te incolumem audiamque Hiberum
narrantem loca, facta, nationes,
ut mos est tuus, applicansque collum
iucundum os oculosque saviabor.
o quantumst hominum beatiorum,　　10
quid me laetius est beatiusve?

X

Varus me meus ad suos amores
visum duxerat e foro otiosum,
scortillum, ut mihi tum repente visumst,
non sane illepidum neque invenustum.
huc ut venimus, incidere nobis　　　5
sermones varii; in quibus, quid esset
iam Bithynia, quo modo se haberet,
ecquonam mihi profuisset aere.
respondi id quod erat, nihil neque ipsis
*nunc praetoribus esse nec cohorti,　　10
cur quisquam caput unctius referret,
praesertim quibus esset irrumator

against your will. But you will be sorry, when your favours are no more desired, ah, poor wretch! what life is left for you? Who now will visit you? to 15 whom will you seem fair? whom now will you love? by whose name will you be called? whom will you kiss? whose lips will you press? But you, Catullus, be resolved and firm.

IX

Veranius, preferred by me to three hundred thousand out of all the number of my friends, have you then come home to your own hearth and your affectionate brothers and your aged mother? You have indeed; O joyful news to me! I shall look 5 upon you safe returned, and hear you telling of the country and its history, the various tribes of the Hiberians, as is your way, and drawing your neck nearer to me I shall kiss your beloved mouth and eyes. O, of all men more blest than others, who is 10 more glad, more blest than I?

X

My dear Varus had taken me from the forum, where I was idling, to pay a visit to his mistress, a little thing, as I thought at a first glance, not at all amiss in manner or looks. When we got there, we 5 fell talking of this and that, and amongst other things, what sort of place Bithynia was now, how its affairs were going on, whether I had made any money there. I answered (what was true) that as things now are neither the praetors themselves nor 10 their staff had found any means of coming back fatter than they went, especially as they had for a

praetor, nec faceret pili cohortem.
'at certe tamen,' inquiunt, 'quod illic
natum dicitur esse, comparasti   15
ad lecticam homines.' ego, ut puellae
unum me facerem beatiorem,
'non' inquam 'mihi tam fuit maligne,
ut, provincia quod mala incidisset,
non possem octo homines parare rectos.'   20
at mi nullus erat nec hic neque illic,
fractum qui veteris pedem grabati
in collo sibi collocare posset.
hic illa, ut decuit cinaediorem,
'quaeso' inquit 'mihi, mi Catulle, paulum   25
istos: commodum enim volo ad Serapim
deferri.' 'mane' inquio puellae;
'istud quod modo dixeram me habere,
fugit me ratio: meus sodalis
Cinnast Gaius; is sibi paravit.   30
verum, utrum illius an mei, quid ad me?
utor tam bene quam mihi *paratis.
sed tu insulsa male ac molesta vivis,
per quam non licet esse neglegentem.'

XI

Furi et Aureli, comites Catulli,
sive in extremos penetrabit Indos,
litus ut longe resonante Eoa
        tunditur unda,
sive in Hyrcanos Arabesque molles,   5
seu Sacas sagittiferosque Parthos,
sive quae septemgeminus colorat
        aequora Nilus,

praetor such a beast, one who did not care a straw
for his subalterns. 'Well, but at any rate' say they,
'you must have got some bearers for your chair. 15
I am told that is the country where they are bred.'
I, to make myself out to the girl as specially
fortunate above the rest, say, 'Things did not go
so unkindly with me—bad as the province was
which fell to my chance—as to prevent my getting 20
eight straight-backed fellows.' Now I had not a
single one, here or there, strong enough to fit to his
shoulder the broken leg of an old sofa. Says she
(just like her shamelessness) 'I beg you, my dear 25
Catullus, lend me those slaves you speak of for a
while; I want just now to be taken to the temple
of Serapis.' 'Stop,' say I to the girl, 'What I said
just now, that I had those slaves—it was a slip—there
is a friend of mine, Gaius Cinna; it was he who bought 30
them for his own use; but it is all one to me whether
they are his or mine, I use them just as if I had
bought them for myself: but you are a most ill-
mannered and tiresome creature, who will not let
one be off one's guard.'

XI

Furius and Aurelius, who will be Catullus' fellow-
travellers, whether he makes his way as far as to the
distant Indies, where the shore is beaten by the far-
resounding eastern wave, or to the Hyrcanians and
soft Arabs, or Sacae and archer Parthians, or the 5
plains which sevenfold Nile discolours, or whether

sive trans altas gradietur Alpes,
Caesaris visens monimenta magni,   10
Gallicum Rhenum, †horribilesque ulti-
     mosque Britannos,
omnia haec, quaecumque feret voluntas
caelitum, temptare simul parati,
pauca nuntiate meae puellae   15
     non bona dicta.
cum suis vivat valeatque moechis,
quos simul complexa tenet trecentos,
nullum amans vere, sed identidem omnium
     ilia rumpens: 20
nec meum respectet, ut ante, amorem,
qui illius culpa cecidit velut prati
ultimi flos, praeter eunte postquam
     tactus aratrost.

XII

Marrucine Asini, manu sinistra
non belle uteris in ioco atque vino:
tollis lintea neglegentiorum.
hoc salsum esse putas? fugit te, inepte:
quamvis sordida res et invenustast.   5
non credis mihi? crede Pollioni
fratri, qui tua furta vel talento
mutari velit: est enim leporum
disertus puer ac facetiarum.
quare aut hendecasyllabos trecentos   10
expecta aut mihi linteum remitte;
quod me non movet aestimatione,
verumst mnemosynum mei sodalis.
nam sudaria Saetaba ex Hiberis
miserunt mihi muneri Fabullus   15
et Veranius: haec amem necessest
ut Veraniolum meum et Fabullum.

he will tramp across the high Alps, to visit the memorials of great Caesar, the Gaulish Rhine, the 10 formidable and remotest Britons,—O my friends, ready as you are to encounter all these risks with me, whatever the will of the gods above shall bring, take a little message, not a kind message, to 15 my mistress. Bid her live and be happy with her paramours, three hundred of whom she holds at once in her embrace, not loving one of them really, but again and again breaking the strength of all. 20 And let her not look to find my love, as before; my love, which by her fault has dropped, like a flower on the meadow's edge, when it has been touched by the plough passing by.

XII

Asinius Marrucinus, you do not make a pretty use of your left hand when we are laughing and drinking; you take away the napkins of people who are off their guard. Do you think this a good joke? You are mistaken, you silly fellow; it is ever 5 so ill-bred, and in the worst taste. You don't believe me? believe your brother Pollio, who would be glad that what you have stolen should be redeemed at the cost of a whole talent: for he is a boy who is a connoisseur of all that is witty and amusing. So now 10 either look out for three hundred hendecasyllables, or send me back my napkin—which does not concern me for what it is worth, but because it is a keepsake from my old friend; for Fabullus and Veranius sent me some Saetaban napkins as a present from Hiberia. 15 How can I help being fond of these, as I am of my dear Veranius and Fabullus?

XIII

Cenabis bene, mi Fabulle, apud me
paucis, si tibi di favent, diebus,
si tecum attuleris bonam atque magnam
cenam, non sine candida puella
et vino et sale et omnibus cachinnis.   5
haec si, inquam, attuleris, venuste noster,
cenabis bene: nam tui Catulli
plenus sacculus est aranearum.
sed contra accipies meros amores
seu quid suavius elegantiusvest: 10
nam unguentum dabo, quod meae puellae
donarunt Veneres Cupidinesque,
quod tu cum olfacies, deos rogabis,
totum ut te faciant, Fabulle, nasum.

XIV

Ni te plus oculis meis amarem,
iucundissime Calve, munere isto
odissem te odio Vatiniano:
nam quid feci ego quidve sum locutus,
cur me tot male perderes poetis?   5
isti di mala multa dent clienti,
qui tantum tibi misit impiorum.
quod si, ut suspicor, hoc novum ac repertum
munus dat tibi Sulla litterator,
non est mi male, sed bene ac beate,   10
quod non dispereunt tui labores.
di magni, horribilem et sacrum libellum,
quem tu scilicet ad tuum Catullum
misti, continuo ut die periret
Saturnalibus, optimo dierum!   15
non non hoc tibi, salse, sic abibit:

XIII

You shall have a good dinner at my house, Fabullus, in a few days, please the gods, if you bring with you a good dinner and plenty of it, not forgetting a pretty girl and wine and wit and all 5 kinds of laughter. If, I say, you bring all this, my charming friend, you shall have a good dinner; for your Catullus' purse is full of cobwebs. But on the other hand you shall have from me love's very essence, or what is sweeter or more delicious than love, if sweeter there be; for I will give you some perfume 10 which the Venuses and Loves gave to my lady; and when you smell it, you will pray the gods to make you, Fabullus, nothing but nose.

XIV

If I did not love you more than my own eyes, my dearest Calvus, I should hate you, as we all hate Vatinius, because of this gift of yours; for what have I done, or what have I said, that you should bring 5 destruction upon me with all these poets? May the gods send down all curses upon that client of yours who sent you such a set of sinners.. But if, as I suspect, this new and choice present is given you by Sulla the schoolmaster, then I am not vexed, but well 10 and happy, because your labours are not lost. Great gods! what a portentous and accursed book! And this was the book which you sent your Catullus, to kill him off at once on the very day of the Saturnalia, 15 best of days. No, no, you rogue, this shall not end

c.   3

nam, si luxerit, ad librariorum
curram scrinia, Caesios, Aquinos,
Suffenum, omnia colligam venena,
ac te his suppliciis remunerabor.   20
vos hinc interea valete abite
illuc, unde malum pedem attulistis,
saecli incommoda, pessimi poetae.

XIV*

Siqui forte mearum ineptiarum
lectores eritis manusque vestras
non horrebitis admovere nobis

  * * * *

XVI

   * * * *

qui me ex versiculis meis putastis,
quod sunt molliculi, parum pudicum.
nam castum esse decet pium poetam
ipsum, versiculos nihil necessest.

XVII

O Colonia, quae cupis ponte ludere longo,
et salire paratum habes, sed vereris inepta
crura ponticuli axulis stantis in redivivis,
ne supinus eat cavaque in palude recumbat;
sic tibi bonus ex tua pons libidine fiat,   5
in quo vel Salisubsili sacra suscipiantur:
munus hoc mihi maximi da, Colonia, risus.
quendam municipem meum de tuo volo ponte
ire praecipitem in lutum per caputque pedesque,
verum totius ut lacus putidaeque paludis   10
lividissima maximeque est profunda vorago.

so for you.   For let the morning only come—I will
be off to the shelves of the booksellers, sweep together Caesii, Aquini, Suffenus, and all such poisonous
stuff, and with these penalties will I pay you back
for your gift.   You poets meantime, farewell, away 20
with you, back to where you brought your cursed feet
from, you plagues of our time, you worst of poets.

XIV* (a fragment)

O my readers—if there be any who will read my
nonsense, and not shrink from touching me with your
hands.   *   *   *   *

XVI (a fragment)

          *   *   *   *

who have supposed me to be immodest, on
account of my verses, because these are rather
voluptuous.   For the holy poet ought to be chaste
himself, his verses need not be.

XVII

Colonia, you who wish to have a long bridge on
which to celebrate your games, and are quite ready
to dance, but fear the ill-jointed legs of your little
bridge, standing as it does on old posts done up
again, lest it should fall sprawling and sink down in
the depths of the marsh ;—so may you have a good 5
bridge made for you according to your desire, one in
which the rites of Salisubsilus himself may be undertaken, as you grant me this gift, Colonia, to make
me laugh my loudest.   There is a townsman of
mine whom I wish to go headlong from your bridge
over head and heels into the mud ;—only let it be 10
where is the blackest and deepest pit of the whole

3—2

insulsissimus est homo, nec sapit pueri instar
bimuli tremula patris dormientis in ulna.
cui cum sit viridissimo nupta flore puella—
et puella tenellulo delicatior haedo,   15
asservanda nigerrimis diligentius uvis,—
ludere hanc sinit ut lubet, nec pili facit uni,
nec se sublevat ex sua parte, sed velut alnus
in fossa Liguri iacet suppernata securi,
tantundem omnia sentiens quam si nulla sit usquam, 20
talis iste meus stupor nil videt, nihil audit,
ipse qui sit, utrum sit an non sit, id quoque nescit.
nunc eum volo de tuo ponte mittere pronum,
si pote stolidum repente excitare veternum
et supinum animum in gravi derelinquere caeno, 25
ferream ut soleam tenaci in voragine mula.

XXII

Suffenus iste, Vare, quem probe nosti,
homost venustus et dicax et urbanus,
idemque longe plurimos facit versus.
puto esse ego illi milia aut decem aut plura
perscripta, nec sic ut fit in palimpsesto   5
relata: chartae regiae, novi libri,
novi umbilici, lora rubra, membranae,
derecta plumbo, et pumice omnia aequata.
haec cum legas tu, bellus ille et urbanus
Suffenus unus caprimulgus aut fossor   10
rursus videtur: tantum abhorret ac mutat.
hoc quid putemus esse? qui modo scurra

bog and stinking marsh. The fellow is a perfect
blockhead, and has not as much sense as a little baby
of two years old sleeping in the rocking arms of his
father. Now whereas he has for a wife a girl in the
freshest flower of youth,—a girl too, more exquisite
than a tender kidling, one who ought to be guarded 15
more diligently than ripest grapes,—he lets her play
as she will, and does not care one straw, and for his
part does not stir himself, but lies like an alder in a
ditch hamstrung by a Ligurian axe, with just as much
perception of everything as if it did not exist any-
where at all. Like this, my booby sees nothing, hears 20
nothing; what he himself is, whether he is or is not,
he does not know so much as this. He it is whom
I want now to send head foremost from your bridge,
to try whether he can all in a moment wake up his
stupid lethargy, and leave his mind sprawling there 25
on its back in the nasty sludge, as a mule leaves her
iron shoe in the sticky mire.

XXII

That Suffenus, Varus, whom you know very
well, is a charming fellow, and has wit and good
manners. He also makes many more verses than
anyone else. I suppose he has got some ten thousand
or even more written out in full, and not, as is often
done, put down on old scraps; imperial paper, new 5
rolls, new bosses, red ties, parchment wrappers; all
ruled with lead and smoothed with pumice. When
you come to read these, the fashionable wellbred
Suffenus I spoke of seems to be nothing but any
goatherd or ditcher, when we look at him again; so 10
absurd and changed he is. How are we to account
for this? The same man who was just now a dinner-

aut siquid hac re †tristius videbatur,
idem infacetost infacetior rure,
simul poemata attigit; neque idem umquam   15
aequest beatus ac poema cum scribit:
tam gaudet in se tamque se ipse miratur.
nimirum idem omnes fallimur, nequest quisquam
quem non in aliqua re videre Suffenum
possis. suus cuique attributus est error: 20
sed non videmus manticae quod in tergost.

XXIII

Furi, cui neque servus est neque arca
nec cimex neque araneus neque ignis,
verumst et pater et noverca, quorum
dentes vel silicem comesse possunt,
est pulcre tibi cum tuo parente   5
et cum coniuge lignea parentis.
nec mirum: bene nam valetis omnes,
pulcre concoquitis, nihil timetis,
non incendia, non graves ruinas,
non furta impia, non dolos veneni,   10
non casus alios periculorum.
atqui corpora sicciora cornu
aut siquid magis aridumst habetis
sole et frigore et esuritione.
quare non tibi sit bene ac beate?   15
a te sudor abest, abest saliva,
mucusque et mala pituita nasi.

haec tu commoda tam beata, Furi,
noli spernere nec putare parvi,
et sestertia quae soles precari   20
centum desine; nam sat es beatus.

table wit or something (if such there be) even more
practised, is more clumsy than the clumsy country,
whenever he touches poetry; and at the same time 15
he is never so complacent as when he is writing a
poem, he delights in himself and admires himself so
much.   True enough, we all are under the same
delusion, and there is no one whom you may not
see to be a Suffenus in one thing or another. Every- 20
body has his own fault assigned to him: but we
do not see that part of the bag which hangs on
our back.

XXIII

Furius, you who have neither a slave, nor a money-
box, nor a bug, nor a spider, nor a fire, but who have
a father and a stepmother too, whose teeth can chew
even a flintstone, you lead a merry life with your 5
father and that dry stick, your father's wife. No
wonder: you all enjoy the best health, your digestions
are excellent, you have nothing to be afraid of; fires,
dilapidations, cruel pilferings, plots to poison you, 10
other chances of danger. And besides this, your
bodies are drier than horn, or drier still if drier
there be, what with sun and cold and fasting.
How can you, Furius, be otherwise than well and
prosperous? You are free from sweat, free from 15
spittle and rheum and tiresome running of the nose.

Since you have such blessings as these, Furius,
do not despise them nor think lightly of them; and
cease to pray, as you do, for the hundred sestertia; 20
for you are quite well off enough as it is.

XXIV

O qui flosculus es Iuventiorum,
non horum modo, sed quot aut fuerunt
aut posthac aliis erunt in annis,
mallem divitias Midae dedisses
isti, cui neque servus est neque arca,   5
quam sic te sineres ab illo amari.
'quid? non est homo bellus?' inquies. est:
sed bello huic neque servus est neque arca.
hoc tu quamlubet abice elevaque:
nec servum tamen ille habet neque arcam.   10

XXV

Cinaede Thalle, mollior cuniculi capillo
vel anseris medullula vel imula oricilla
                                        situque araneoso,
idemque Thalle, turbida rapacior procella,
cum †diva mulier aries† ostendit oscitantes,   5
remitte pallium mihi meum, quod involasti,
sudariumque Saetabum catagraphosque Thynos,
inepte, quae palam soles habere tamquam avita.
quae nunc tuis ab unguibus reglutina et remitte,
ne laneum latusculum manusque mollicellas   10
inusta turpiter tibi flagella conscribillent,
et insolenter aestues velut minuta magno
deprensa navis in mari vesaniente vento.

XXVI

Furi, villula nostra non ad Austri
flatus oppositast neque ad Favoni
nec saevi Boreae aut Apheliotae,
verum ad milia quindecim et ducentos.
o ventum horribilem atque pestilentem!   5

XXIV

You who are the flower of the Juventii, not only of those we know, but of all who either have been or shall be hereafter in other years,—I had rather you had given the riches of Midas to that fellow who has neither servant nor money-box, than so allow your- 5 self to be liked by him. 'What? is he not a gentle- man?' you will say. O yes; but this gentleman has neither a servant nor a money-box. You may put this aside and make as little of it as you like: still, he has neither a servant nor a money-box. 10

XXV

Effeminate Thallus, softer than rabbit's fur or down of goose or lap of ear, or dusty cobweb; and also, Thallus, more violent than a wild storm when † † Send me back my cloak which you 5 have pounced upon, and my Saetaban napkin and Bithynian tablets, you silly fellow, which you keep by you openly, as if they were heirlooms. Unglue and let drop these at once from your claws, lest your soft downy flanks and pretty tender hands should have 10 ugly figures branded and scrawled on them by the whip, and lest you should toss about as you are little used to do, like a tiny boat caught in the vast sea, when the wind is raging wildly.

XXVI

Furius, my little farm stands exposed not to the blasts of Auster nor Favonius nor fierce Boreas or Apheliotes, but to a call of fifteen thousand two hundred sesterces. A wind that brings horror and 5 pestilence!

XXVII

Minister vetuli puer Falerni
inger mi calices amariores,
ut lex Postumiae iubet magistrae,
ebrioso acino ebriosioris.
at vos quolubet hinc abite, lymphae,   5
vini pernicies, et ad severos
migrate: hic merus est Thyonianus.

XXVIII

Pisonis comites, cohors inanis
aptis sarcinulis et expeditis,
Verani optime tuque mi Fabulle,
quid rerum geritis? satisne cum isto
vappa frigoraque et famem tulistis?   5
ecquidnam in tabulis patet lucelli
expensum, ut mihi, qui meum secutus
praetorem refero datum lucello

    pete nobiles amicos!
at vobis mala multa di deaeque   10
dent, opprobria Romuli Remique.

XXIX

Quis hoc potest videre, quis potest pati,
nisi impudicus et vorax et aleo,
Mamurram habere quod Comata Gallia
habebat *ante et ultima Britannia?
cinaede Romule, haec videbis et feres?   5
[es impudicus et vorax et aleo.]
et ille nunc superbus et superfluens
perambulabit omnium cubilia
ut albulus columbus aut †ydoneus?

XXVII

Come boy, you who serve out the old Falernian, fill up stronger cups for me, as the law of Postumia, mistress of the revels, ordains, Postumia more drunken than a drunken grape. But water, begone, away with 5 you, water, destruction of wine, and take up your abode with scrupulous folk. This is the pure juice of the Thyonian god.

XXVIII

You subalterns of Piso, a needy train, with baggage handy and easily carried, my excellent Veranius and you my Fabullus, how are you? have you borne cold and hunger with that windbag long enough? is there any gain, however small, to be 5 seen in your tablets, entered as paid out, as there is in mine, who after following in my praetor's train put down on the credit side   . So much for running after powerful friends! But may the gods and god- 10 desses bring many curses upon you, you blots on the names of Romulus and Remus.

XXIX

Who can look upon this, who can suffer this, except he be shameless and voracious and a gambler, that Mamurra should have what Gallia Comata and furthest Britain had once? Debauched Romulus, 5 will you see and endure this? [You are shameless and voracious and a gambler.] And shall he now, proud and full to overflowing, make a progress through the beds of all, like a white cock pigeon or †   ?

cinaede Romule, haec videbis et feres?   10
es impudicus et vorax et aleo.
eone nomine, imperator unice,
fuisti in ultima occidentis insula,
ut ista vostra diffututa Mentula
ducenties comesset aut trecenties?   15
quid est alid sinistra liberalitas?
parum expatravit an parum helluatus est?
paterna prima lancinata sunt bona:
secunda praeda Pontica: inde tertia
Hibera, quam scit amnis aurifer Tagus.   20
†hunc Galliae timet et Britanniae†
quid hunc malum fovetis? aut quid hic potest,
nisi uncta devorare patrimonia?
eone nomine urbis †opulentissime
socer generque, perdidistis omnia?   25

XXX

Alfene immemor atque unanimis false sodalibus,
iam te nil miseret, dure, tui dulcis amiculi?
iam me prodere, iam non dubitas fallere, perfide?
num facta impia fallacum hominum caelicolis placent?
quae tu neglegis, ac me miserum deseris in malis;   5
eheu quid faciant, dic, homines, cuive habeant fidem?
certe tute iubebas animam tradere, inique, me
inducens in amorem, quasi tuta omnia mi forent.
idem nunc retrahis te ac tua dicta omnia factaque
ventos irrita ferre ac nebulas aerias sinis.   10
si tu oblitus es, at di meminerunt, meminit Fides,
quae te ut paeniteat postmodo facti faciet tui.

Debauched Romulus, will you see and endure 10
this? You are shameless and voracious and a
gambler. Was it this then, you one and only
general, that took you to the furthest island of the
West? was it that that worn-out profligate of yours,
Mentula, should devour twenty or thirty millions? 15
What else then, if this be not, is perverted liberality?
His ancestral property was first torn to shreds;
then came his prize-money from Pontus, then in the
third place that from the Hiberus, which the gold- 20
bearing river Tagus knows all about. And him do the
Gauls and Britains fear? Why do you both support
this scoundrel? or what can he do but devour rich
patrimonies? Was it for this †   † that you, 25
father-in-law and son-in-law, have ruined everything?

XXX

Alfenus, ungrateful and false to your faithful
comrades, do you henceforward (ah cruel!) not pity
your beloved friend?—henceforward not shrink from
betraying me, deceiving me, faithless one? Do the
deeds of deceivers please the gods above?—All this
you disregard, and desert me in my sorrow and 5
trouble; ah, tell me, what are men to do, whom are
they to trust? For truly you used to bid me trust my
soul to you (ah unjust!), leading me into love as if
all were safe for me; you, who now draw back from
me, and let the winds and vapours of the air bear 10
away all your words and deeds unratified. If you
have forgotten this, yet the gods remember it, remembers Faith, who will soon make you repent of
your deed.

XXXI

Paene insularum, Sirmio, insularumque
ocelle, quascumque in liquentibus stagnis
marique vasto fert uterque Neptunus,
quam te libenter quamque laetus inviso,
vix mi ipse credens Thyniam atque Bithynos   5
liquisse campos et videre te in tuto.
o quid solutis est beatius curis
cum mens onus reponit, ac peregrino
labore fessi venimus larem ad nostrum
desideratoque acquiescimus lecto?   10
hoc est, quod unumst pro laboribus tantis.
salve, o venusta Sirmio, atque ero gaude:
gaudete vosque, o Lydiae lacus undae:
ridete, quicquid est domi cachinnorum.

XXXII

Amabo, mea dulcis Ipsithilla,
meae deliciae, mei lepores,
iube ad te veniam meridiatum.
et si iusseris, illud adiuvato,
nequis liminis obseret tabellam,   5
neu tibi lubeat foras abire.

verum, siquid ages, statim iubeto
    .   .   .   .   .   .

XXXIII

O furum optime balneariorum
Vibenni pater et cinaede fili,

cur non exilium malasque in oras
itis, quandoquidem patris rapinae
notae sunt populo?   5

XXXI

Sirmio, bright eye of peninsulas and islands, all
that in liquid lakes or vast ocean either Neptune
bears: how willingly and with what joy I revisit
you, scarcely trusting myself that I have left Thynia
and the Bithynian plains, and that I see you in safety. 5
Ah, what is more blessed than to put cares away,
when the mind lays by its burden, and tired with
labour of far travel we have come to our own home
and rest on the couch we longed for. This it is 10
which alone is worth all these toils. Welcome,
lovely Sirmio, and rejoice in your master, and rejoice ye too, waters of the Lydian lake, and laugh
out aloud whatever laughter you have in the depths
of your home.

XXXII

I entreat you, my sweet Ipsithilla, my darling,
my charmer, bid me to come and rest at noonday
with you. And if you do bid me, grant me this
kindness too, that no one may bar the panel of your
threshold, nor you yourself choose to go away, but 5
stay at home   . But if you will at all, then
bid me come at once . . . .

XXXIII

Cleverest of all clothes-stealers at the baths, father
Vibennius and you his profligate son,   off
with you into banishment and the dismal regions,
since the father's plunderings are known to all the
world   5

XXXIV

Dianae sumus in fide
puellae et pueri integri:
[Dianam pueri integri]
  puellaeque canamus.

o Latonia, maximi   5
magna progenies Iovis,
quam mater prope Deliam
  deposivit olivam,

montium domina ut fores
silvarumque virentium   10
saltuumque reconditorum
  amniumque sonantum.

tu Lucina dolentibus
Iuno dicta puerperis,
tu potens Trivia et notho's   15
  dicta lumine Luna.

tu cursu, dea, menstruo
metiens iter annuum
rustica agricolae bonis
  tecta frugibus exples.   20

sis quocumque tibi placet
sancta nomine, Romulique,
antique ut solita's, bona
  sospites ope gentem.

XXXV

Poetae tenero, meo sodali
velim Caecilio, papyre, dicas
Veronam veniat, Novi relinquens
Comi moenia Lariumque litus:
nam quasdam volo cogitationes   5
amici accipiat sui meique.
quare, si sapiet, viam vorabit,

XXXIV

We girls and chaste boys are lieges of Diana.
Diana let us sing, chaste boys and girls. O child of
Latona, great offspring of greatest Jove, whom thy 5
mother laid down by the Delian olive-tree, that thou
mightest be the lady of mountains and green woods, 10
and sequestered glens and sounding rivers; thou art
called Juno Lucina by mothers in pains of travail,
thou art called mighty Trivia and Moon with 15
counterfeit light. Thou, goddess, measuring out the
year with monthly course, fillest full with goodly
fruits the rustic home of the husbandman. Be thou 20
hallowed by whatever name thou wilt; and as of old
thou wert wont, with good help keep safe the race of
Romulus.

XXXV

I ask you, papyrus leaf, to tell the gentle poet,
my friend Caecilius, to come to Verona, leaving the
walls of Novum Comum and the shore of Larius:
for I wish him to receive certain thoughts of a friend 5
of his and mine. Wherefore if he is wise he will

quamvis candida miliens puella
euntem revocet manusque collo
ambas iniciens roget morari ;   10
quae nunc, si mihi vera nuntiantur,
illum deperit impotente amore :
nam quo tempore legit incohatam
Dindymi dominam, ex eo misellae
ignes interiorem edunt medullam.   15
ignosco tibi, Sapphica puella
Musa doctior : est enim venuste
Magna Caecilio incohata Mater.

XXXVI

Annales Volusi, cacata charta,
votum solvite pro mea puella :
nam sanctae Veneri Cupidinique
vovit, si sibi restitutus essem
desissemque truces vibrare iambos,   5
electissima pessimi poetae
scripta tardipedi deo daturam
infelicibus ustulanda lignis.
et haec pessima se puella vidit
iocosis lepide vovere divis.   10
nunc, o caeruleo creata ponto,
quae sanctum Idalium Uriosque apertos
quaeque Ancona Gnidumque harundinosam
colis quaeque Amathunta quaeque Golgos
quaeque Durachium Hadriae tabernam,   15
acceptum face redditumque votum,
si non illepidum neque invenustumst.
at vos interea venite in ignem,
pleni ruris et infacetiarum
annales Volusi, cacata charta.   20

devour the way with haste, though his fair lady
should call him back a thousand times, and throwing
both her arms round his neck beg him to delay. She 10
now, if a true tale is brought to me, dotes on him
with passionate love. For since she read the beginning of his *Lady of Dindymus*, ever since then,
poor girl, the fires have been wasting her inmost
marrow. I can feel for you, maiden more scholarly 15
than the Sapphic muse; for Caecilius has indeed
made a lovely beginning to his *Magna Mater*.

XXXVI

Chronicle of Volusius, dirty waste paper, discharge
a vow on behalf of my love; for she vowed to holy
Venus and to Cupid that if I were restored to her
love and ceased to dart fierce iambics, she would 5
give to the lamefooted god the choicest writings of
the worst of poets, to be burnt with wood from
some accursed tree: and the lady saw that these were
the 'worst poems' that she was vowing to the merry
gods in pleasant sport. Now therefore, O thou whom 10
the blue sea bare, who inhabitest holy Idalium and
open Urii, who dwellest in Ancona and reedy Cnidus
and in Amathus and in Golgi, and in Dyrrhachium
the meeting-place of all Hadria, enter the vow as 15
received and duly paid, so surely as it is not out of
taste nor inelegant. Meantime come you here into
the fire, full of rusticity and clumsiness, chronicle of
Volusius, dirty waste paper.   20

XXXVIII

Malest, Cornifici, tuo Catullo,
malest, me hercule, et [ei] laboriose,
et magis magis in dies et horas.
quem tu, quod minimum facillimumquest,
qua solatus es allocutione?   5
irascor tibi. sic meos amores?
paulum quid lubet allocutionis,
maestius lacrimis Simonideis.

XXXIX

Egnatius, quod candidos habet dentes,
renidet usquequaque. si ad rei ventumst
subsellium, cum orator excitat fletum,
renidet ille. si ad pii rogum fili
lugetur, orba cum flet unicum mater,   5
renidet ille. quicquid est, ubicumquest,
quodcumque agit, renidet. hunc habet morbum,
neque elegantem, ut arbitror, neque urbanum.
quare monendum te est mihi, bone Egnati.
si urbanus esses aut Sabinus aut Tiburs   10
aut parcus Umber aut obesus Etruscus
aut Lanuvinus ater atque dentatus
aut Transpadanus, ut meos quoque attingam,
aut quilubet, qui puriter lavit dentes,
tamen renidere usquequaque te nollem: 15
nam risu inepto res ineptior nullast.

.   .   .   .

XL

quaenam te mala mens, miselle Ravide,
agit praecipitem in meos iambos?
quis deus tibi non bene advocatus
vecordem parat excitare rixam?

XXXVIII

Your Catullus is ill, Cornificius, ill and in distress, and that more and more daily and hourly. And you, the lightest and easiest task, with what cheering word have you consoled him? I am getting angry with 5 you—what, treat my love so? Give me only some little word of comfort, something as moving as the tears of Simonides!

XXXIX

Egnatius, because he has white teeth, is ever-lastingly smiling. If people come to the prisoner's bench, when the counsel for the defence is making everyone cry, he smiles: if they are wailing at the funeral of an affectionate son, when the bereaved 5 mother is weeping for her only boy, he smiles: whatever it is, wherever he is, whatever he is doing, he smiles: it is a malady he has, neither an elegant one as I think, nor in good taste. So I must give you a bit of advice, my good Egnatius. If you were 10 a Roman or a Sabine or a Tiburtine or a thrifty Umbrian or a plump Etruscan, or a black and tusky Lanuvian, or a Transpadane (to touch on my own people too), or anybody else who washes his teeth with clean water, still I should not like you to be 15 smiling everlastingly; for there is nothing more silly than a silly laugh.   .   .   .   .

XL

What infatuation, my poor Ravidus, drives you headlong in the way of my iambics? What god invoked by you amiss is going to stir up a senseless

an ut pervenias in ora vulgi?   5
quid vis? qualubet esse notus optas?
eris, quandoquidem meos amores
cum longa voluisti amare poena.

XLI

Ameana
tota milia me decem poposcit,
ista turpiculo puella naso,
decoctoris amica Formiani.
propinqui, quibus est puella curae,   5
amicos medicosque convocate:
non est sana puella, nec rogare
qualis sit solet aes imaginosum.

XLII

Adeste, hendecasyllabi, quot estis
omnes undique, quotquot estis omnes.
iocum me putat esse moecha turpis,
et negat mihi vestra reddituram
pugillaria, si pati potestis.   5
persequamur eam, et reflagitemus.
quae sit, quaeritis. illa, quam videtis
turpe incedere, mimice ac moleste
ridentem catuli ore Gallicani.
circumsistite eam, et reflagitate,   10
'moecha putida, redde codicillos,
redde, putida moecha, codicillos.'
non assis facis? o lutum, lupanar,
aut si perditius potes quid esse.
sed non est tamen hoc satis putandum.   15
quod si non aliud †potest, ruborem
ferreo canis exprimamus ore:
conclamate iterum altiore voce

quarrel? Is it that you wish to be talked about? 5
What do you want? would you be known no matter
how? So you shall, since you have chosen to love
my lady,—and long shall you rue it.

XLI

Ameana   asked me for a round ten thousand;
that girl with the ugly nose, the mistress of the
bankrupt of Formiae. You relations, who have the
charge of the girl, call together friends and doctors: 5
the girl is not right in her mind, and never asks
the looking-glass what she is like.

XLII

Hither from all sides, hendecasyllables, as many
as there are of you, all of you as many as there are.
An ugly drab thinks she may jest with me, and says
she will not give me back your tablets, if you can 5
submit to that. Let us follow her, and demand them
back again. You ask who she is. That one whom
you see strutting with an ugly gait, grinning like a
vulgar mountebank with the gape of a Cisalpine
hound. Stand round her and call for them back 10
again. 'Dirty drab, give back the tablets, give back
the tablets, dirty drab!' Don't you care a penny for
that? O, filth, O beastliness! or anything else that
I can call you filthier still! But we must not think 15
this enough. Well, if nothing else can do it, let us
force a blush from the brazen face of the beast: call

'moecha putida, redde codicillos,
redde, putida moecha, codicillos.'   20
sed nil proficimus, nihil movetur.
mutandast ratio modusque nobis,
siquid proficere amplius potestis:
'pudica et proba, redde codicillos.'

XLIII

Salve, nec minimo puella naso
nec bello pede nec nigris ocellis
nec longis digitis nec ore sicco
nec sane nimis elegante lingua,
decoctoris amica Formiani.   5
ten Provincia narrat esse bellam?
tecum Lesbia nostra comparatur?
o saeclum insapiens et infacetum!

XLIV

O funde noster, seu Sabine seu Tiburs,
(nam te esse Tiburtem autumant, quibus non est
cordi Catullum laedere: at quibus cordist,
quovis Sabinum pignore esse contendunt)
sed seu Sabine sive verius Tiburs,   5
fui libenter in tua suburbana
villa, malamque pectore expuli tussim,
non immerenti quam mihi meus venter,
dum sumptuosas appeto, dedit, cenas.
nam, Sestianus dum volo esse conviva,   10
orationem in Antium petitorem
plenam veneni et pestilentiae legi.
hic me gravedo frigida et frequens tussis
quassavit usque dum in tuum sinum fugi
et me recuravi otioque et urtica.   15

out again with louder voice, 'Dirty drab, give back the tablets, give back the tablets, dirty drab!' We do no 20 good: she does not mind. We must change our plan and method, if you can do better so—'Maiden modest and chaste, give back the tablets.'

XLIII

I greet you, lady, you who neither have a tiny nose, nor a pretty foot, nor black eyes, nor long fingers, nor dry mouth, nor indeed a very refined tongue, mistress of the bankrupt of Formiae. Is it 5 you who are pretty, as the Province tells us? is it with you that our Lesbia is compared? O, this age! how tasteless and illbred it is!

XLIV

My farm, whether Sabine or Tiburtine (for those affirm that you are Tiburtine, who do not love to annoy Catullus, but those who do will wager anything that you are Sabine)—but at all events, whether you are Sabine or more rightly Tiburtine, 5 I was glad to be in your retreat, 'twixt country and town, and to clear my chest of the troublesome cough, which my greediness gave me (not undeservedly) whilst I was running after costly feasts. I wanted to go to dinner with Sestius, and so I read 10 a speech of his against the candidate Antius, full of poison and plague. Thereupon a shivering chill and a constant cough shook me to pieces, till at last I fled to your bosom, and set myself right again by a diet 15

c. 6

quare refectus maximas tibi grates
ago, meum quod non es ulta peccatum.
nec deprecor iam, si nefaria scripta
Sesti recepso, quin gravedinem et tussim
non mi, sed ipsi Sestio ferat frigus,   20
qui tunc vocat me, cum malum librum legi.

XLV

Acmen Septimius suos amores
tenens in gremio 'mea' inquit 'Acme,
ni te perdite amo atque amare porro
omnes sum assidue paratus annos
quantum qui pote plurimum perire,   5
solus in Libya Indiaque tosta
caesio veniam obvius leoni.'
hoc ut dixit, Amor, sinistra, †ut ante†
dextra, sternuit approbationem.
at Acme leviter caput reflectens   10
et dulcis pueri ebrios ocellos
illo purpureo ore saviata
'sic' inquit 'mea vita Septimille,
huic uni domino usque serviamus,
ut multo mihi maior acriorque   15
ignis mollibus ardet in medullis.'
hoc ut dixit, Amor, sinistram ut ante,
dextram sternuit approbationem.
nunc ab auspicio bono profecti
mutuis animis amant amantur.   20
unam Septimius misellus Acmen
mavolt quam Syrias Britanniasque:
uno in Septimio fidelis Acme
facit delicias libidinesque.
quis ullos homines beatiores   25
vidit, quis Venerem auspicatiorem?

of laziness and nettle broth. So now, having re-
covered, I return you my best thanks because you
did not punish my error. And henceforth, if I ever
again take in hand the abominable writings of Sestius
I freely consent that the chill shall bring catarrh
and cough, not upon me, but upon Sestius himself, 20
for inviting me just when I have read a stupid book.

XLV

Septimius, holding in his bosom his darling Acme,
says, 'My Acme, if I do not love thee to desperation,
and if I am not ready to go on loving thee continually
through all my years as much as he who can love most 5
desperately, may I in Libya or sunburnt India meet a
green-eyed lion alone.' As he said this, Love on the
left, as before on the right, sneezed goodwill. Then
Acme, slightly bending back her head, kissed with 10
that rosy mouth her sweet love's swimming eyes,
and said, 'So, my life, my darling Septimius, may we
ever serve this one master, so surely as (I swear) more 15
strongly and fiercely than ever burns for me the flame
in my melting marrow.' As she said this, Love, as
before on the left, now on the right sneezed goodwill.
And now, setting out from a good omen, heart in heart 20
they live, loving and loved. Poor Septimius prefers
Acme alone to Syrias and Britains. In Septimius,
him alone, his faithful Acme takes her fill of loves
and pleasures. Who ever saw human beings more 25
blest? Who ever saw a more fortunate love?

XLVI

Iam ver egelidos refert tepores,
iam caeli furor aequinoctialis
iucundis Zephyri silescit auris.
linquantur Phrygii, Catulle, campi
Niceaeque ager uber aestuosae: 5
ad claras Asiae volemus urbes.
iam mens praetrepidans avet vagari,
iam laeti studio pedes vigescunt.
o dulces comitum valete coetus,
longe quos simul a domo profectos   10
diversae variae viae reportant.

XLVII

Porci et Socration, duae sinistrae
Pisonis, scabies famesque munda,
vos Veraniolo meo et Fabullo
verpus praeposuit Priapus ille?
vos convivia lauta sumptuose   5
de die facitis? mei sodales
quaerunt in trivio vocationes?

XLVIII

Mellitos oculos tuos, Iuventi,
siquis me sinat usque basiare,
usque ad milia basiem trecenta,
nec mi umquam videar satur futurus,
non si densior aridis aristis   5
sit nostrae seges osculationis.

XLVI

Now spring brings back balmy warmth, now the glad gales of Zephyr are hushing the rage of the equinoctial sky. Deserted be the Phrygian plains, Catullus, and the rich land of burning Nicaea: away 5 let us fly to the renowned cities of Asia. Now my soul flutters in anticipation and yearns to stray; now my eager feet rejoice and grow strong. Farewell, dear bands of fellow travellers, who set out together 10 from your far away home, and whom divided ways through changing scenes are bringing back again.

XLVII

Porcius and Socration, Piso's two left hands, you plague and mere famine, has that obscene Priapus preferred you to my dear Veranius and Fabullus? Are you spending money and holding splendid rich 5 banquets at vast expense in broad daylight, whilst my old friends must hunt in the streets for an invitation?

XLVIII

Your honeyed eyes, Juventius, if one should let me go on kissing still, I would kiss them three hundred thousand times, nor would I think I should ever have enough, no, not if the harvest of our kissing 5 were thicker than the ripe ears of corn.

XLIX

Disertissime Romuli nepotum,
quot sunt quotque fuere, Marce Tulli,
quotque post aliis erunt in annis,
gratias tibi maximas Catullus
agit pessimus omnium poeta,   5
tanto pessimus omnium poeta
quanto tu optimus omnium's patronus.

L

Hesterno, Licini, die otiosi
multum lusimus in †meis tabellis,
ut convenerat esse delicatos.
scribens versiculos uterque nostrum
ludebat numero modo hoc modo illoc,   5
reddens mutua per iocum atque vinum.
atque illinc abii tuo lepore
incensus, Licini, facetiisque,
ut nec me miserum cibus iuvaret
nec somnus tegeret quiete ocellos,   10
sed toto indomitus furore lecto
versarer, cupiens videre lucem,
ut tecum loquerer simulque ut essem.
at defessa labore membra postquam
semimortua lectulo iacebant,   15
hoc, iucunde, tibi poema feci,
ex quo perspiceres meum dolorem.
nunc audax cave sis, precesque nostras
oramus cave despuas, ocelle,
ne poenas Nemesis reposcat a te.   20
est vemens dea: laedere hanc caveto.

XLIX

Most skilled in speech of the descendants of
Romulus, all who are, and all who have been, and
all who shall be hereafter in other years, Marcus
Tullius,—to thee his warmest thanks Catullus gives,
the worst of all poets ; as much the worst poet of all 5
as you are the best advocate of all.

L

Yesterday, Licinius, we made holiday and played
many a game with my tablets, as we had agreed to
take our pleasure. Each of us pleased his fancy in
writing verses, now in one metre, now in another, 5
answering each other, as we laughed and drank
our wine. I came away from this so fired by your
cleverness and humour, Licinius, that my food did not
ease my pain, and sleep spread no rest over my eyes, 10
but raging with frenzy I tossed about all over my
bed, longing to see the dawn, that I might talk to you
and be with you. But when my limbs were worn
out with fatigue and lay half-dead on my couch, 15
I made this poem for you, my sweet friend, that from
it you might learn my pains. Now be not too proud,
and do not, I pray you, apple of my eye, do not
reject my prayers, lest Nemesis demand penalties 20
from you in turn. She is a mighty goddess—beware
of offending her.

LI a

Ille mi par esse deo videtur,
ille, si fas est, superare divos,
qui sedens adversus identidem te
    spectat et audit
dulce ridentem, misero quod omnis   5
eripit sensus mihi; nam simul te,
Lesbia, aspexi, nihil est super mi
    [vocis in ore]
lingua sed torpet, tenuis sub artus
flamma demanat, sonitu suopte   10
tintinant aures, gemina teguntur
    lumina nocte.

LI b

Otium, Catulle, tibi molestumst:
otio exultas nimiumque gestis.
otium et reges prius et beatas
    perdidit urbes.

LII

Quid est, Catulle? quid moraris emori?
sella in curuli struma Nonius sedet,
per consulatum perierat Vatinius:
quid est, Catulle? quid moraris emori?

LIII

Risi nescio quem modo e corona,
qui, cum mirifice Vatiniana
meus crimina Calvus explicasset,
admirans ait haec manusque tollens,
'di magni, salaputtium disertum!'   5

LI a

He seems to me to be equal to a god, he, if it may be, seems to surpass the very gods, who sitting opposite thee again and again gazes at thee and hears thee sweetly laughing. Such a thing takes 5 away my senses, alas! for whenever I see thee, Lesbia, at once no voice at all remains within my mouth, but my tongue falters, a subtle flame steals secretly through my limbs, my ears tingle with inward 10 humming, my eyes are quenched in twofold night.

LI b (a fragment)

Idleness, Catullus, does you harm, you riot in your idleness and wanton too much. Idleness ere now has ruined both kings and wealthy cities.

LII

What is it, Catullus? why do you not make haste to die? That wen Nonius sits in the curule chair; Vatinius forswears himself by his consulship. What is it, Catullus? why do you not make haste to die?

LIII

A fellow in the crowd made me laugh just now: when my dear Calvus had drawn out in splendid style his accusations against Vatinius, he lifted up his hands in wonder and 'Great gods (says he), what 5 an eloquent manikin!'

LIV

Otonis caput (oppidost pusillum)
† et Eri rustice † semilauta crura,

si non omnia, displicere vellem
tibi et Fuficio seni recocto.

LIV b

*   *   *   *

Irascere iterum meis iambis
immerentibus, unice imperator.

LV

Oramus, si forte non molestumst,
demonstres, ubi sint tuae tenebrae.
te campo quaesivimus minore,
te in circo, te in omnibus libellis,
te in templo summi Iovis sacrato;   5
in Magni simul ambulatione
femellas omnes, amice, prendi,
quas vultu vidi tamen sereno.
† a, vel te sic ipse † flagitabam,
'Camerium mihi, pessimae puellae!'   10
quaedam inquit, nudum reduc[ta pectus],
'en hic in roseis latet papillis.'
sed te iam ferre Herculi labos est.   13
non custos si fingar ille Cretum,   23
non si Pegaseo ferar volatu,
non Ladas [si] ego pinnipesve Perseus,   25
non Rhesi niveae citaeque bigae:
adde huc plumipedas volatilesque,
ventorumque simul require cursum;
quos iunctos, Cameri, [ut] mihi dicares,
defessus tamen omnibus medullis   30
et multis langoribus peresus

LIV

Otho's head (very small it is) and your half-washed legs, rustic Erius   these points at least, if not all about them, I should wish to be disliked by you and Fuficius, that old fellow renewed to youth again.

LIV b (a fragment)

*   *   *   *

You will again be angered by my iambics, my innocent iambics, you one and only general.

LV

I beg you, if I may without offence, show me where is your dark corner. I have looked for you in the lesser Campus, in the Circus, in all the book-sellers' shops, in the hallowed temple of great Jove. 5 At the same time, in the portico of Magnus, I caught hold of all the girls, my friend, who nevertheless faced me with untroubled look. Ah, even so I myself kept asking them for you 'Give me my Camerius, you wicked girls!' One of them, baring her naked 10 bosom, says 'Look here, he is hiding between my rosy breasts.' Well, to bear with you is now a labour 13 of Hercules. Not though I should be moulded in 23 brass like the fabled warder of Crete, not though I were borne aloft like flying Pegasus, not if I were Ladas or wingfooted Perseus, not if I were the swift 25 snow-white pair of Rhesus could I overtake you: add to these the feather-footed gods and those that fly, and with them call for the swiftness of the winds; though you should harness all these, Camerius, and press them into my service, yet I should be tired 30 out in my very marrow, and worn away with many

essem te, mi amice, quaeritando.   32
tanto ten fastu negas, amice?   14
dic nobis ubi sis futurus, ede   15
audacter, committe, crede luci.
num te lacteolae tenent puellae?
si linguam clauso tenes in ore,
fructus proicies amoris omnes:
verbosa gaudet Venus loquella.   20
vel si vis, licet obseres palatum,
dum vestri sim particeps amoris.

LVI

O rem ridiculam, Cato, et iocosam
dignamque auribus et tuo cachinno.
ride, quidquid amas, Cato, Catullum:
res est ridicula et nimis iocosa.

     ·   ·   ·   ·

LVII

Pulcre convenit improbis cinaedis,
Mamurrae pathicoque Caesarique.
nec mirum: maculae pares utrisque,
urbana altera et illa Formiana,
impressae resident nec eluentur: 5
morbosi pariter, gemelli utrique,
uno in lectulo erudituli ambo,

rivales socii puellularum.
pulcre convenit improbis cinaedis.   10

LVIII

Caeli, Lesbia nostra, Lesbia illa,
illa Lesbia, quam Catullus unam
plus quam se atque suos amavit omnes,
nunc in quadriviis et angiportis
     magnanimi Remi nepotes.   5

faintings, my friend, while searching for you. Do 32
you deny yourself so haughtily, my friend? Tell 15
us where you are likely to be, out with it boldly,
trust me with it, give it to the light. Do the milkwhite maids detain you? If you keep your tongue
shut up within your mouth, you will waste all the
gains of love ; Venus loves an utterance full of words. 20
However, if you will, you may lock up your lips, so
long as you let me be a sharer in your love.

LVI

O, Cato, what an absurdly funny thing, worthy
for you to hear and laugh at. Laugh, as much as
you love Catullus, Cato. The thing is too absurd
and funny   ·   ·   ·   ·

LVII

Well agreed are the abominable profligates,
Mamurra the effeminate, and Caesar—no wonder
either. Like blots on each, one from the city and
one from Formiae, are deeply impressed, and will 5
never be washed out. Diseased alike, very twins,
both on one sofa, dilettante writers, rivals and part-
ners in love. Well agreed are the abominable
profligates.   10

LVIII

O, Caelius, my Lesbia, that Lesbia, Lesbia whom
alone Catullus loved more than himself and all his
own, now in the crossroads and alleys serves the 5
filthy lusts of the descendants of lordly-minded
Remus.

LIX

Bononiensis Rufa
uxor Meneni, saepe quam in sepulcretis
vidistis ipso rapere de rogo cenam,
cum devolutum ex igne prosequens panem
ab semiraso tunderetur ustore.   5

LX

Num te leaena montibus Libystinis
aut Scylla latrans infima inguinum parte
tam mente dura procreavit ac taetra,
ut supplicis vocem in novissimo casu
contemptam haberes, a nimis fero corde?   5

LXI

Collis o Heliconii
cultor, Uraniae genus,
qui rapis teneram ad virum
virginem, o Hymenaee Hymen,
    o Hymen Hymenaee,   5

cinge tempora floribus
suave olentis amaraci,
flammeum cape, laetus huc
huc veni niveo gerens
    luteum pede soccum,   10

excitusque hilari die,
nuptialia concinens
voce carmina tinnula,
pelle humum pedibus, manu
    pineam quate taedam.   15

LIX

Rufa of Bononia　　　the wife of Menenius, she whom you have often seen in the graveyards grabbing the baked meats from the very pyre, when as she ran after the loaf rolling down out of the fire she was thumped by the half-shaved slave of the under- 5 taker.

LX

Was it a lioness from Libyan mountains or a Scylla barking from her womb below that bare you, you that are so hard-hearted and monstrous as to hold in contempt your suppliant's voice in his last need, ah, too cruel-hearted one? 5

LXI

Haunter of the Heliconian mount, Urania's son, thou who bearest away the tender maid to her bridegroom, O Hymenaeus Hymen, O Hymen Hymenaeus! 5
Bind thy brows with the flowers of sweet marjoram, put on the marriage veil, hither, hither merrily come, bearing on thy foot the yellow shoe, 10
and wakened on this joyful day, singing with resonant voice the nuptial songs, strike the ground with thy feet, shake with thy hand the pine torch. 15

namque Vinia Manlio,
qualis Idalium colens
venit ad Phrygium Venus
iudicem, bona cum bona
  nubet alite virgo,   20

floridis velut enitens
myrtus Asia ramulis,
quos Hamadryades deae
ludicrum sibi rosido
  nutriunt umore.   25

quare age huc aditum ferens
perge linquere Thespiae
rupis Aonios specus,
nympha quos super irrigat
  frigerans Aganippe,   30

ac domum dominam voca
coniugis cupidam novi,
mentem amore revinciens,
ut tenax edera huc et huc
  arborem implicat errans.   35

vosque item simul, integrae
virgines, quibus advenit
par dies, agite in modum
dicite 'o Hymenaee Hymen,
  o Hymen Hymenaee.'   40

ut lubentius, audiens
se citarier ad suum
munus, huc aditum ferat
dux bonae Veneris, boni
  coniugator amoris.   45

For now shall Vinia wed with Manlius, Vinia as fair
as Venus who dwells in Idalium, when she came to the
Phrygian judge; a good maiden with a good omen,   20

like the Asian myrtle shining with flowering
sprays, which the Hamadryad goddesses with dewy
moisture nourish as a plaything for themselves.   25

Hither then, come hither, haste to leave the
Aonian caves of the Thespian rock, which the
nymph Aganippe cooling besprinkles from above;   30

and call to her home the lady of the house, full
of desire for her new husband, binding her heart with
love, as the clinging ivy here and there straying
clasps the tree.   35

Ye too with me, unwedded virgins, for whom a
like day is coming, come, in measure say, O Hymenaeus Hymen, O Hymen Hymenaeus!   40

that hearing himself summoned to his own office,
hither more readily may come the herald of chaste
Venus, the coupler of chaste love.   45

quis deus magis est † ama-
tis petendus amantibus?
quem colent homines magis
caelitum? o Hymenaee Hymen,
    o Hymen Hymenaee.   50

te suis tremulus parens
invocat, tibi virgines
zonula soluunt sinus,
te timens cupida novus
    captat aure maritus.   55

tu fero iuveni in manus
floridam ipse puellulam
dedis a gremio suae
matris, o Hymenaee Hymen,
    o Hymen Hymenaee.   60

nil potest sine te Venus,
fama quod bona comprobet,
commodi capere: at potest
te volente. quis huic deo
    compararier ausit?   65

nulla quit sine te domus
liberos dare, nec parens
stirpe nitier: at potest
te volente. quis huic deo
    compararier ausit?   70

quae tuis careat sacris,
non queat dare praesides
terra finibus: at queat
te volente. quis huic deo
    compararier ausit?   75

What god is more worthy to be invoked by lovers who are loved? whom of the heavenly ones shall men worship more than thee? O Hymenaeus Hymen, O Hymen Hymenaeus!　　　　　50

Thee for his children the aged father invokes, for thee the maidens loose their robes from the girdle: for thee the new husband listens fearfully with eager ear.　　　　　55

Thou thyself givest into the hands of the fiery youth the blooming maiden from the bosom of her mother, O Hymenaeus Hymen, O Hymen Hymenaeus!　　　　　60

No pleasure can Venus take without thee, such as honest fame may approve; but can, if thou art willing. What god dare match himself with this god? 65

No house without thee can give children, no parent rest on his offspring; but can, if thou art willing. What god dare match himself with this god?　　　　　70

A land that should want thy sanctities would not be able to produce guardians for its borders—but could, if thou wert willing. What god dare match himself with this god?　　　　　75

claustra pandite ianuae,
virgo † adest. viden ut faces
splendidas quatiunt comas?
       *   *   *
tardet ingenuus pudor:
       *   *   *
quem tamen magis audiens   80
   flet, quod ire necesse est.   81

flere desine. non tibi, Au-   86
runculeia, periculumst,
nequa femina pulcrior
clarum ab Oceano diem   85
   viderit venientem.   96

talis in vario solet
divitis domini hortulo
stare flos hyacinthinus.
sed moraris, abit dies: 90
   [prodeas, nova nupta.]

prodeas, nova nupta, si
iam videtur, et audias
nostra verba. víde ut faces
aureas quatiunt comas: 95
   prodeas, nova nupta.

non tuus levis in mala
deditus vir adultera
probra turpia persequens
a tuis teneris volet   100
   secubare papillis,

lenta *qui velut adsitas
vitis implicat arbores,
implicabitur in tuum
complexum. sed abit dies: 105
   prodeas, nova nupta.

Throw open the fastenings of the door; the
bride is coming. See you how the torches shake
their shining tresses? *   * noble shame delays. 80
*   * Yet listening rather to this, she weeps for 81
that she must go.

Cease to weep. Not to you, Aurunculeia, is there 86
danger that any fairer woman shall see the bright 85
day coming from ocean.   96

So in the painted garden of a rich owner stands a
hyacinth flower—but you delay, the day is passing; 90
come forth, new bride.

Come forth, new bride, if now you will, and hear
our words. See how the torches shake their golden 95
tresses!—come forth, new bride.

Your husband will not, lightly given to some
wicked paramour, following shameful ways of dis- 100
honour, wish to lie apart from your soft breast.

As the pliant vine entwines the trees planted
near it, so will he be entwined in your embrace.
But the day is passing; come forth, new bride. 105

tollite, o pueri, faces:
flammeum video venire.
ite, concinite in modum
'io Hymen Hymenaee io,   120
    io Hymen Hymenaee.'

ne diu taceat procax
Fescennina iocatio,
    *   *   *

en tibi domus ut potens
et beata viri tui,
quae tibi sine serviat
(io Hymen Hymenaee io,   155
    io Hymen Hymenaee),

usque dum tremulum movens
cana tempus anilitas
omnia omnibus annuit.
io Hymen Hymenaee io,   160
    io Hymen Hymenaee.

transfer omine cum bono
limen aureolos pedes,
rasilemque subi forem.
io Hymen Hymenaee io,   165
    io Hymen Hymenaee.

aspice, intus ut accubans
vir tuus Tyrio in toro
totus immineat tibi.
io Hymen Hymenaee io,   170
    io Hymen Hymenaee.

Raise aloft the torches, boys : I see the wedding veil coming. Go on, sing in measure, Io Hymen 120 Hymenaeus io, io Hymen Hymenaeus ! Let not the merry Fescennine raillery be silent long.

* * * * *

See how mighty and rich for you is the house of your husband ; be content to be mistress here, (Io Hymen Hymenaeus io, io Hymen Hymenaeus !) 155 even till hoary old age, shaking a trembling head, nods assent to all for all. Io Hymen Hymenaeus io, 160 io Hymen Hymenaeus !

Bear over the threshold with a good omen your golden feet, and enter the polished door. Io Hymen 165 Hymenaeus io, io Hymen Hymenaeus !

See how your husband within, reclining on the purple couch, is all eagerness for you. Io Hymen Hymenaeus io, io Hymen Hymenaeus !   170

illi non minus ac tibi
pectore uritur intimo
flamma, sed penite magis.
io Hymen Hymenaee io,   175
    io Hymen Hymenaee.

mitte bracchiolum teres,
praetextate, puellulae :
iam cubile adeat viri.
io Hymen Hymenaee io,   180
    io Hymen Hymenaee.

vos bonae senibus viris
cognitae bene feminae,
collocate puellulam.
io Hymen Hymenaee io,   185
    io Hymen Hymenaee.

iam licet venias, marite :
uxor in thalamo tibist
ore floridulo nitens,
alba parthenice velut   190
    luteumve papaver.

at, marite, (ita me iuvent
caelites) nihilo minus
pulcher es, neque te Venus
neglegit. sed abit dies :   195
    perge, ne remorare.

non diu remoratus es,
iam venis. bona te Venus
iuverit, quoniam palam
quod cupis capis et bonum   200
    non abscondis amorem.

In his inmost heart no less than in yours burns the flame, but deeper within. Io Hymen Hymenaeus io, io Hymen Hymenaeus! 175

Let go, young boy, the smooth arm of the maiden, let her now come to her husband's bed. Io Hymen Hymenaeus io, io Hymen Hymenaeus! 180

Ye, good women, well wedded to ancient husbands, set the maiden in her place. Io Hymen Hymenaeus io, io Hymen Hymenaeus! 185

Now you may come, husband : your wife is in the bridechamber, shining with flowery face, like a white 190 daisy or yellow poppy.

But, husband, so help me the gods, you are no less beautiful, nor does Venus neglect you. But the 195 day is passing. Go on then, delay not.

Not long have you delayed. Already you come. May chaste Venus help you, since openly you take 200 your desire and do not hide your honest love.

ille pulveris Africi
siderumque micantium
subducat numerum prius,
qui vostri numerare vult   205
   multa milia ludi.

ludite ut lubet, et brevi
liberos date. non decet
tam vetus sine liberis
nomen esse, sed indidem   210
   semper ingenerari.

Torquatus volo parvulus
matris e gremio suae
porrigens teneras manus
dulce rideat ad patrem   215
   semihiante labello.

sit suo similis patri
Manlio et facile *omnibus
noscitetur ab insciis
et pudicitiam suae   220
      matris indicet ore.

talis illius a bona
matre laus genus approbet,
qualis unica ab optima
matre Telemacho manet   225
   fama Penelopeo.

claudite ostia, virgines:
lusimus satis. at, boni
coniuges, bene vivite et
munere assiduo valentem   230
   exercete iuventam.

Let him first count up the number of the dust of Africa and of the glittering stars, who would number 205 the many thousands of your joys.

Sport as ye will, and soon give birth to children. It is not fit that so old a name should be without children, but that they should be ever born from the 210 same stock.

I would see a little Torquatus, stretching his baby hands from his mother's bosom, smile a sweet smile 215 at his father with half-open lip.

May he be like his father Manlius, and easily be recognised by all, even those who do not know, and 220 declare by his face the fair fame of his mother.

May such honour, coming from his chaste mother, approve his descent, as for Telemachus son of Penelope remains unparagoned the honour derived from 225 his noble mother.

Maidens, shut the doors. We have sported enough. But ye, happy pair, live happily, and in your office 230 exercise joyously your vigorous youth.

LXII

Vesper adest, iuvenes, consurgite: Vesper Olympo
expectata diu vix tandem lumina tollit.
surgere iam tempus, iam pinguis linquere mensas;
iam veniet virgo, iam dicetur Hymenaeus.

    Hymen o Hymenaee, Hymen ades o Hymenaee!

cernitis, innuptae, iuvenes? consurgite contra;   6
nimirum Oetaeos ostendit Noctifer ignes.
sic certest; viden ut perniciter exiluere?
non temere exiluere, canent quod † visere par est.

    Hymen o Hymenaee, Hymen ades o Hymenaee!

non facilis nobis, aequales, palma paratast;   11
aspicite, innuptae secum ut meditata requirunt.
non frustra meditantur, habent memorabile quod sit.
nec mirum, penitus quae tota mente laborent.
nos alio mentes, alio divisimus aures: 15
iure igitur vincemur, amat victoria curam.
quare nunc animos saltem committite vestros;
dicere iam incipient, iam respondere decebit.

    Hymen o Hymenaee, Hymen ades o Hymenaee!

Hespere, qui caelo fertur crudelior ignis?   20
qui natam possis complexu avellere matris,
complexu matris retinentem avellere natam,
et iuveni ardenti castam donare puellam.
quid faciunt hostes capta crudelius urbe?

    Hymen o Hymenaee, Hymen ades o Hymenaee!

LXII

Youths. The evening is come, rise up, ye youths. Vesper from Olympus now at last is just raising his long looked-for light. Now is it time to rise, now to leave the rich tables ; now will come the bride, now will the Hymen-song be sung. Hymen, O Hymenaeus, Hymen, be present, O Hymenaeus ! 5

Maidens. See ye, maidens, the youths ? Rise up to meet them. For sure the night star shews his Oetaean fires. So it is indeed ; see you how nimbly they have sprung up ? it is not for nothing that they have sprung up : they will sing something which it is worth while to look at. Hymen, O Hymenaeus, Hymen, be present, O Hymenaeus ! 10

Youths. No easy palm is set out for us, comrades ; look how the maidens are conning what they have learnt. Not in vain do they learn, they have something worth remembering ; no wonder, since they labour deeply with their whole mind. We have distracted elsewhere our thoughts, elsewhere our ears ; 15 fairly then shall we be beaten ; victory loves care. Wherefore now at least match your minds with theirs. Anon they will begin to speak, anon it will be fitting for us to answer. Hymen, O Hymenaeus, Hymen, be present, O Hymenaeus !

Maidens. Hesperus, what more cruel fire moves 20 in the sky? for thou canst endure to tear the daughter from her mother's embrace, from her mother's embrace to tear the clinging daughter, and give the chaste maiden to the burning youth. What more cruel than this do enemies when a city falls? Hymen, O Hymenaeus, Hymen, be present, O Hymenaeus !

Hespere, qui caelo lucet iucundior ignis?   26
qui desponsa tua firmes conubia flamma,
quae pepigere viri, pepigerunt ante parentes,
nec iunxere prius quam se tuus extulit ardor.
quid datur a divis felici optatius hora?   30

    Hymen o Hymenaee, Hymen ades o Hymenaee!

*   *   *   *

Hesperus e nobis, aequales, abstulit unam.

*   *   *   *

namque tuo adventu vigilat custodia semper.
nocte latent fures, quos idem saepe revertens,
Hespere, mutato comprendis nomine Eous.   35

    [Hymen o Hymenaee, Hymen ades o Hymenaee!]

*   *   *   *

at lubet innuptis ficto te carpere questu.
quid tum, si carpunt, tacita quem mente requirunt?

    Hymen o Hymenaee, Hymen ades o Hymenaee!

ut flos in saeptis secretus nascitur hortis,
ignotus pecori, nullo convulsus aratro,   40
quem mulcent aurae, firmat sol, educat imber,

*   *   *   *

multi illum pueri, multae optavere puellae:
idem cum tenui carptus defloruit ungui,
nulli illum pueri, nullae optavere puellae:
sic virgo dum intacta manet, dum cara suis est; 45
cum castum amisit polluto corpore florem,
nec pueris iucunda manet nec cara puellis.

    Hymen o Hymenaee, Hymen ades o Hymenaee!

Youths. Hesperus, what more welcome fire shines 26 in the sky? for thou with thy flame confirmest the contracted espousals, which husbands and parents have promised beforehand, but have not united till thy flame has arisen. What is given by the gods 30 more desirable than the fortunate hour? Hymen, O Hymenaeus, Hymen, be present, O Hymenaeus!

* * * *

Maidens. Hesperus, friends, has taken away one of us...

* * * *

Youths. For at thy coming the guard is always awake. By night thieves hide themselves, whom thou, Hesperus, often overtakest returning, Hesperus the same but with changed name Eous. [Hymen, O 35 Hymenaeus, Hymen, be present, O Hymenaeus!]

* * * *

But girls love to chide thee with feigned complaint. What then, if they chide him whom they desire in their secret heart? Hymen, O Hymenaeus, Hymen, be present, O Hymenaeus!

Maidens. As a flower springs up secretly in a fenced garden, unknown to the cattle, torn up by no 40 plough, which the winds caress, the sun strengthens, the shower draws forth, many boys, many girls, desire it; when the same flower fades, nipped by a sharp nail, no boys, no girls, desire it: so a maiden, whilst she remains untouched, so long she is dear to her 45 own; when she has lost her chaste flower with sullied body, she remains neither lovely to boys nor dear to girls. Hymen, O Hymenaeus, Hymen, be present, O Hymenaeus!

ut vidua in nudo vitis quae nascitur arvo
numquam se extollit, numquam mitem educat uvam,
sed tenerum prono deflectens pondere corpus   51
iam iam contingit summum radice flagellum ;
hanc nulli agricolae, nulli coluere iuvenci.
at si forte eademst ulmo coniuncta marita,
multi illam agricolae, multi coluere iuvenci :   55
sic virgo dum intacta manet, dum inculta senescit ;
cum par conubium maturo tempore adeptast,
cara viro magis et minus est invisa parenti.

   [Hymen o Hymenaee, Hymen ades o Hymen-
       aee !]   58[b]

at tu ne pugna cum tali coniuge, virgo.
non aequumst pugnare, pater cui tradidit ipse,   60
ipse pater cum matre, quibus parere necessest.
virginitas non tota tuast, ex parte parentumst ;
tertia pars patrist, pars est data tertia matri,
tertia sola tuast : noli pugnare duobus,
qui genero sua iura simul cum dote dederunt.   65

   Hymen o Hymenaee, Hymen ades o Hymenaee !

LXIII

Super alta vectus Attis celeri rate maria
Phrygium ut nemus citato cupide pede tetigit
adiitque opaca silvis redimita loca deae,
stimulatus ibi furenti rabie, vagus animi,
devolvit ili acuto sibi pondera silice.   5

Youths.   As a widowed vine which grows up in a bare field never raises itself aloft, never brings forth a mellow grape, but bending its tender form with 50 downward weight, even now touches the root with the topmost twig; no farmers, no oxen till it: but if it chance to be joined in marriage to the elm, many farmers, many oxen till it.   So a maid, whilst she 55 remains untouched, so long is she aging untilled; but when in ripe season she has gained an equally matched marriage, she is more dear to her husband and less distasteful to her father.   [Hymen, O 58ᵇ Hymenaeus, Hymen, be present, O Hymenaeus!]

But you, maiden, strive not with such a husband; it is not right to strive with him to whom your father 60 himself gave you, your father himself with your mother, whom you must obey.

Your maidenhead is not all your own; partly it belongs to your parents, a third part is given to your father, a third part to your mother, only the third is yours; do not contend with two, who have given their rights to their son-in-law together with the 65 dowry.   Hymen, O Hymenaeus, Hymen, be present, O Hymenaeus!

LXIII

Borne in his swift bark over deep seas, Attis, when eagerly with rapid foot he reached the Phrygian forest, and entered the goddess's shadowy abodes crowned with woods; there, urged by raging madness, bewildered in mind, he cast down from him with sharp flint-stone the burden of his members. 5

c.   10

itaque ut relicta sensit sibi membra sine viro,
etiam recente terrae sola sanguine maculans
niveis citata cepit manibus leve typanum,
typanum, †tubam Cybelles†, tua, Mater, initia,
quatiensque terga tauri teneris cava digitis   10
canere haec suis adortast tremebunda comitibus.
'agite ite ad alta, Gallae, Cybeles nemora simul,
simul ite, Dindymenae dominae vaga pecora,
aliena quae petentes *celere exules loca
sectam meam executae duce me mihi comites   15
rapidum salum tulistis truculentaque pelage
et corpus evirastis Veneris nimio odio,
hilarate *erae citatis erroribus animum.
mora tarda mente cedat; simul ite, sequimini
Phrygiam ad domum Cybelles, Phrygia ad nemora
      deae,   20
ubi cymbalum sonat vox, ubi tympana reboant,
tibicen ubi canit Phryx curvo grave calamo,
ubi capita Maenades vi iaciunt ederigerae,
ubi sacra sancta acutis ululatibus agitant,
ubi suevit illa divae volitare vaga cohors: 25
quo nos decet citatis celerare tripudiis.'
simul haec comitibus Attis cecinit notha mulier,
thiasus repente linguis trepidantibus ululat,
leve tympanum remugit, cava cymbala recrepant,
viridem citus adit Idam properante pede chorus.   30
furibunda simul anhelans vaga vadit, animam agens,
comitata tympano Attis per opaca nemora dux,
veluti iuvenca vitans onus indomita iugi:
rapidae ducem sequuntur Gallae properipedem.
itaque ut domum Cybelles tetigere lassulae,   35

So when he felt his limbs to have lost their man-
hood, and yet with fresh blood dabbling the face of
the ground, swiftly with snowy hands she seized the
light timbrel, timbrel, trumpet of Cybele, thy mysteries, Mother, and shaking with soft fingers the
hollow ox-hide thus began she to sing to her com- 10
panions tremulously: 'Come away, ye Gallae, go to
the deep forests of Cybele together, together go,
wandering herd of the lady of Dindymus, who swiftly
seeking alien homes as exiles, following my band as
I led you in my train, have endured the fast-flowing 15
brine and the raging seas, and have unmanned
your bodies from utter hatred of love, cheer your
Lady's heart with swift wanderings. Let slow delay
depart from your mind; go together, follow to the
Phrygian house of Cybele, to the Phrygian forests 20
of the goddess, where the noise of cymbals sounds,
where timbrels re-echo, where the Phrygian flute-
player blows a deep note on his curved reed, where
the Maenads ivy-crowned toss their heads violently,
where with shrill yells they shake the holy emblems,
where that wandering company of the goddess is 25
wont to rove, whither for us 'tis meet to hasten with
rapid dances.'

So soon as Attis, woman yet no true one, sang
this to her attendants, the revellers suddenly with
quivering tongues yell aloud, the light timbrel rings
again, clash again the hollow cymbals, swift to
green Ida goes the rout with hurrying foot. Then 30
too frenzied, panting, uncertain, wanders, gasping for
breath, attended by the timbrel, Attis, through the
dark forests their leader, as a heifer unbroken starting
aside from the burden of the yoke. Fast follow the
Gallae their hurrying leader. So when they gained
the house of Cybele, faint and weary, after much toil 35

nimio e labore somnum capiunt sine Cerere.
piger his labante langore oculos sopor operit:
abit in quiete molli rabidus furor animi.
sed ubi oris aurei Sol radiantibus oculis
lustravit aethera album, sola dura, mare ferum,   40
pepulitque noctis umbras vegetis sonipedibus,
ibi Somnus excitum Attin fugiens citus abiit:
trepidante eum recepit dea Pasithea sinu.
ita de quiete molli rapida sine rabie
simul ipse pectore Attis sua facta recoluit,   45
liquidaque mente vidit sine quis ubique foret,
animo aestuante rusum reditum ad vada tetulit.
ibi maria vasta visens lacrimantibus oculis,
patriam allocuta maestast ita voce miseriter.
'patria o mei creatrix, patria o mea genetrix,   50
ego quam miser relinquens, dominos ut erifugae
famuli solent, ad Idae tetuli nemora pedem,
ut apud nivem et ferarum gelida stabula forem
et earum †omnia adirem† furibunda latibula?
ubinam aut quibus locis te positam, patria, reor? 55
cupit ipsa pupula ad te sibi derigere aciem,
rabie fera carens dum breve tempus animus est.
egone a mea remota haec ferar in nemora domo?
patria, bonis, amicis, genitoribus abero?
abero foro, palaestra, stadio et guminasiis?   60
miser a miser, querendumst etiam atque etiam, anime.
quod enim genus figuraest, ego non quod habuerim?
ego †mulier, ego adolescens, ego ephebus, ego puer,
ego guminasi fui flos, ego eram decus olei:
mihi ianuae frequentes, mihi limina tepida,   65

they take their rest without bread; heavy sleep covers
their eyes with drooping weariness, in soft slumber
departs the raging madness of their mind.   But when
the sun with the flashing eyes of his golden face
lightened the clear heaven, the spaces of hard earth, 40
the wild sea, and chased away the shades of night
with eager tramping steeds refreshed, then Sleep fled
from wakened Attis and quickly was gone; him the
goddess Pasithea received in her fluttering bosom.
So after soft slumber, free from violent madness, as
soon as Attis himself in his heart reviewed his own 45
deed, and saw with clear mind without what and
where he was, with surging mind again he sped
back to the waves.   There, looking out upon the
waste seas with streaming eyes, thus did she
piteously address her country with tearful voice.
'O my country that gavest me life! O my country 50
that barest me! leaving whom, ah wretch! as run-
away servants leave their masters, I have borne my
foot to the forests of Ida, to live among snows and
frozen lairs of wild beasts, and visit in my frenzy all
their lurking-dens,—where then or in what region do
I think thy place to be, O my country?   Mine eye- 55
balls unbidden long to turn their gaze to thee, while
for a short space my mind is free from wild frenzy.
I, shall I from my own home be borne far away
into these forests? from my country, my possessions,
my friends, my parents, shall I be absent? absent
from the market, the wrestling-place, the race-course, 60
the playground? unhappy, ah unhappy heart, again,
again must thou complain.   For what form of human
figure is there which I had not? I, to be a woman—!
I who was a stripling, I a youth, I a boy, I was the
flower of the playground, I was once the glory of the
palaestra: mine were crowded doorways, mine warm 65

mihi floridis corollis redimita domus erat,
linquendum ubi esset orto mihi sole cubiculum.
ego nunc deum ministra et Cybeles famula ferar?
ego Maenas, ego mei pars, ego vir sterilis ero?
ego viridis algida Idae nive amicta loca colam?   70
ego vitam agam sub altis Phrygiae columinibus
ubi cerva silvicultrix, ubi aper nemorivagus?
iam iam dolet quod egi, iam iamque paenitet.'
   Roseis ut huic labellis sonitus * citus abiit *,
geminas deorum ad aures nova nuntia referens,   75
ibi iuncta iuga resolvens Cybele leonibus
laevumque pecoris hostem stimulans ita loquitur.
'agedum' inquit 'age ferox [i], fac ut hunc furor
    [agitet],
fac uti furoris ictu reditum in nemora ferat,
mea libere nimis qui fugere imperia cupit.   80
age caede terga cauda, tua verbera patere,
fac cuncta mugienti fremitu loca retonent,
rutilam ferox torosa cervice quate iubam.'
ait haec minax Cybelle religatque iuga manu.
ferus ipse sese adhortans rapidum incitat animo,   85
vadit, fremit, refringit virgulta pede vago.
at ubi umida albicantis loca litoris adiit,
tenerumque vidit Attin prope marmora pelagi,
facit impetum: ille demens fugit in nemora fera:
ibi semper omne vitae spatium famula fuit.   90
dea magna, dea Cybelle, dea domina Dindymi,
procul a mea tuus sit furor omnis, era, domo:
alios age incitatos, alios age rabidos.

thresholds, mine the flowery garlands to deck my house when I was to leave my chamber at sunrise. I, shall I now be called—what? a handmaid of the gods, a ministress of Cybele? I a Maenad, I part of myself, a barren man shall I be? shall I dwell in icy snow-clad regions of verdant Ida, I pass my life 70 under the high summits of Phrygia, with the hind that haunts the woodland, with the boar that ranges the forest? now, now I rue my deed, now, now I wish it undone.' From his rosy lips as thus the voice came quickly forth, bringing a new message to both ears of 75 the gods, then Cybele loosening the fastened yoke from her lions, and goading that terror of the herd who drew on the left, thus speaks: 'Come then,' she says, 'come, go fiercely, let madness hunt him hence, bid him hence by stroke of madness hie him to the forests again, him who would be too free, and escape 80 from my sovereignty. Come, lash back with tail, endure thy own blows, make all around resound with bellowing roar, shake fiercely the ruddy mane on thy brawny neck.' Thus says wrathful Cybele, and with her hand unbinds the yoke. The monster stirs himself and rouses him to fury of heart; he speeds 85 away, he roars, he breaks the brushwood with ranging foot. But when he came to the watery stretches of the white-gleaming shore, and saw tender Attis by the smooth spaces of the sea, he rushes at him— madly flies Attis to the wild woodland. There always for all the space of his life was he a handmaid. 90

Goddess, great goddess, Cybele, goddess, lady of Dindymus, far from my house be all thy fury, O my queen; others drive thou in frenzy, others drive to madness.

LXIV

Peliaco quondam prognatae vertice pinus
dicuntur liquidas Neptuni nasse per undas
Phasidos ad fluctus et fines Aeeteos,
cum lecti iuvenes, Argivae robora pubis,
auratam optantes Colchis avertere pellem   5
ausi sunt vada salsa cita decurrere puppi,
caerula verrentes abiegnis aequora palmis;
diva quibus retinens in summis urbibus arces
ipsa levi fecit volitantem flamine currum,
pinea coniungens inflexae texta carinae.   10
illa rudem cursu prima imbuit Amphitriten.
quae simul ac rostro ventosum proscidit aequor,
tortaque remigio spumis incanduit unda,
emersere † feri candenti e gurgite vultus
aequoreae monstrum Nereides admirantes.   15
illa * siqua alia viderunt luce marinas
mortales oculis nudato corpore Nymphas
nutricum tenus extantes e gurgite cano.
tum Thetidis Peleus incensus fertur amore,
tum Thetis humanos non despexit hymenaeos,   20
tum Thetidi pater ipse iugandum Pelea sensit.
o nimis optato saeclorum tempore nati
heroes, salvete, deum * gens, o bona matrum
progenies salvete, iterum * salvete bonarum *.   23ᵃ
vos ego saepe meo vos carmine compellabo:
teque adeo eximie taedis felicibus aucte,   25
Thessaliae columen Peleu, cui Iuppiter ipse,
ipse suos divum genitor concessit amores.

LXIV

Pinetrees of old, born on the top of Pelion, are said to have swum through the liquid waters of Neptune to the waves of Phasis and the realms of Aeetes, when the chosen youths, the flower of Argive strength, desiring to bear away from the Colchians the golden fleece, dared to course over 5 the salt seas with swift ship, sweeping the blue expanse with fir-wood blades, for whom the goddess who holds the fortresses of city-tops made with her own hands the car flitting with light breeze, binding the piny structure of the bowed keel. That ship first 10 hanselled with voyage Amphitrite untried before.

So when she ploughed with her beak the windy expanse, and the wave churned by the oars grew white with foam-flakes, forth looked, wild visages, from the foaming tide the Nereids of the deep wondering at the strange thing. On that day, if on 15 any other, mortals saw with their eyes the sea-Nymphs standing forth from the hoary tide naked as far as the paps. Then is Peleus said to have caught fire with love of Thetis, then did Thetis not disdain mortal espousals, then the Father himself 20 knew in his heart that Peleus must be joined to Thetis. O ye, in happiest time of ages born, hail, heroes, sprung from gods! hail, kindly offspring of good mothers, hail again! you often in my song, 23ᵃ you will I address. And specially thee, greatly blessed by fortunate marriage torches, pillar of 25 Thessaly, Peleus, to whom Jupiter himself, the king of the gods himself granted his own Love. Thee

tene Thetis tenuit pulcherrima Nereine?
tene suam Tethys concessit ducere neptem,
Oceanusque, mari totum qui amplectitur orbem?   30
  Quis simul optatae finito tempore luces
advenere, domum conventu tota frequentat
Thessalia, oppletur laetanti regia coetu :
dona ferunt prae se, declarant gaudia voltu.
deseritur *Cieros, linquunt Phthiotica Tempe,   35
Crannonisque domos ac moenia Larisaea,
Pharsalum coeunt, Pharsalia tecta frequentant.
rura colit nemo, mollescunt colla iuvencis,
non humilis curvis purgatur vinea rastris,
non falx attenuat frondatorum arboris umbram,   41
non glaebam prono convellit vomere taurus,   40
squalida desertis rubigo infertur aratris.
ipsius at sedes, quacumque opulenta recessit
regia, fulgenti splendent auro atque argento.
candet ebur soliis, collucent pocula mensae,   45
tota domus gaudet regali splendida gaza.
pulvinar vero divae geniale locatur
sedibus in mediis, Indo quod dente politum
tincta tegit roseo conchyli purpura fuco.
  Haec vestis priscis hominum variata figuris   50
heroum mira virtutes indicat arte.
namque fluentisono prospectans litore Diae
Thesea cedentem celeri cum classe tuetur
indomitos in corde gerens Ariadna furores ;
necdum etiam sese quae visit visere credit,   55
ut pote fallaci quae tum primum excita somno
desertam in sola miseram se cernat harena.
immemor at iuvenis fugiens pellit vada remis,

did fairest Thetis clasp, daughter of Nereus? to thee did Tethys grant to wed her granddaughter, and Oceanus, who circles all the world with sea? 30

Now when that longed-for day in time fulfilled had come for them, all Thessaly in full assembly crowds the house, the palace is thronged with a joyful company. They bring gifts in their hands, they display joy in their looks. Cieros is deserted; they leave Phthiotic Tempe and the houses of 35 Crannon and the walls of Larissa; at Pharsalus they meet, and flock to the houses of Pharsalus. None now tills the lands; the necks of the steers grow soft; no more is the ground of the vineyard cleared with curved rakes; no more does the pruners' 41 hook thin the shade of the tree; no more does the ox tear up the soil with downward share; rough rust 40 creeps over the deserted ploughs. But Peleus' own abodes, so far as inward stretched the wealthy palace, shine with glittering gold and silver. White gleams the ivory of the thrones, bright shine the cups on the 45 table; the whole house is gay and gorgeous with royal treasure. But see, the royal marriage bed is being set for the goddess in the midst of the palace, smoothly fashioned of Indian tusk, covered with purple of the shell tinged with rosy stain.

This coverlet, broidered with shapes of ancient 50 men, with wondrous art sets forth the worthy deeds of heroes. For there, looking forth from the wave-sounding shore of Dia, Ariadna sees Theseus, as he sails away with swift fleet, Ariadna bearing uncurbed madness in her heart. Not yet can she believe she beholds what yet she does behold; since 55 now, now first wakened from treacherous sleep she sees herself, poor wretch, deserted on the lonely sand. Meanwhile the youth flies and strikes the

irrita ventosae linquens promissa procellae.
quem procul ex alga maestis Minois ocellis   60
saxea ut effigies bacchantis prospicit, eheu,
prospicit et magnis curarum fluctuat undis,
non flavo retinens subtilem vertice mitram,
non contecta levi velatum pectus amictu,
non tereti strophio lactentis vincta papillas,   65
omnia quae toto delapsa e corpore passim
ipsius ante pedes fluctus salis adludebant.
sed neque tum mitrae neque tum fluitantis amictus
illa vicem curans toto ex te pectore, Theseu,
toto animo, tota pendebat perdita mente.   70
a misera, assiduis quam luctibus externavit
spinosas Erycina serens in pectore curas
illa *ex tempestate, ferox quo tempore Theseus
egressus curvis e litoribus Piraei
attigit iniusti regis Cortynia templa.   75
    Nam perhibent olim crudeli peste coactam
Androgeoneae poenas exsolvere caedis
electos iuvenes simul et decus innuptarum
Cecropiam solitam esse dapem dare Minotauro.
quis angusta malis cum moenia vexarentur,   80
ipse suum Theseus pro caris corpus Athenis
proicere optavit potius quam talia Cretam
funera Cecropiae nec funera portarentur;
atque ita nave levi nitens ac lenibus auris
magnanimum ad Minoa venit sedesque superbas.   85
hunc simul ac cupido conspexit lumine virgo
regia, quam suavis expirans castus odores
lectulus in molli complexu matris alebat,
quales Eurotae progignunt flumina myrtus
aurave distinctos educit verna colores,   90
non prius ex illo flagrantia declinavit

waters with his oars, leaving unfulfilled his empty
pledges to the windy storm; at whom afar from 60
the weedy beach with streaming eyes the daughter
of Minos, like a marble figure of a bacchanal, looks
forth, alas, looks forth, tempest-tost with great tides
of passion. Nor does she still keep the delicate coif
on her golden head, nor has her veiled breast covered
with her light raiment, nor her milkwhite bosom bound 65
with the smooth girdle; all these, as they slipt off
around her whole form, before the maiden's very feet
the salt waves lapped. She for her headgear then, she
for her floating raiment then, cared not, but on thee,
Theseus, with all her thoughts, with all her soul, with 70
all her mind (lost, ah lost!) was hanging, unhappy
maid! whom with unceasing floods of grief Erycina
maddened, sowing thorny cares in her breast, even
from that season, what time bold Theseus setting
forth from the winding shores of Piraeus reached
the Gortynian palace of the lawless king.   75

For they tell how of old, driven by a cruel pestilence to pay a penalty for the death of Androgeos,
Cecropia was wont to give as a meal to the Minotaur
chosen youths, and with them the flower of unwedded
maids. Now when the crowded walls were troubled 80
by these evils, Theseus himself for his dear Athens
chose to offer his own body, rather than that such
deaths, living deaths, of Cecropia should be borne
to Crete. Thus then, speeding his course with light
bark and gentle gales, he comes to lordly Minos and 85
his haughty halls. Him when the maiden beheld
with eager eye, the princess, whom her chaste couch
breathing sweet odours still nursed in her mother's
soft embrace, like myrtles which spring by the streams
of Eurotas, or the varied colours which the breath of 90
spring draws forth, she turned not her burning eyes

lumina, quam cuncto concepit corpore flammam
funditus atque imis exarsit tota medullis.
heu misere exagitans immiti corde furores
sancte puer, curis hominum qui gaudia misces,   95
quaeque regis Golgos quaeque Idalium frondosum,
qualibus incensam iactastis mente puellam
fluctibus in flavo saepe hospite suspirantem!
quantos illa tulit languenti corde timores!
†quanto saepe magis fulgore expalluit auri;   100
cum saevum cupiens contra contendere monstrum
aut mortem appeteret Theseus aut praemia laudis.
non ingrata tamen frustra munuscula divis
promittens tacito †succendit vota labello.
nam velut in summo quatientem bracchia Tauro   105
quercum aut conigeram sudanti cortice pinum
indomitus turbo contorquens flamine robur
eruit (illa procul radicitus exturbata
prona cadit, late *casu cuncta* obvia frangens),
sic domito saevum prostravit corpore Theseus   110
nequiquam vanis iactantem cornua ventis.
inde pedem sospes multa cum laude reflexit
errabunda regens tenui vestigia filo,
ne labyrintheis e flexibus egredientem
tecti frustraretur inobservabilis error.   115
    Sed quid ego a primo digressus carmine plura
commemorem, ut linquens genitoris filia vultum,
ut consanguineae complexum, ut denique matris,
quae misera in gnata deperdita †leta,
omnibus his Thesei dulcem praeoptarit amorem,   120
aut ut vecta ratis spumosa ad litora Diae,
aut ut eam [molli] devinctam lumina somno
liquerit immemori discedens pectore coniunx?
saepe illam perhibent ardenti corde furentem

away from him, till she had caught fire in all her
heart deep within, and glowed all flame in her inmost marrow.   Ah! thou that stirrest cruel madness
with ruthless heart, divine boy, who minglest joys of 95
men with cares, and thou, who reignest over Golgi
and leafy Idalium, with what tides did ye toss the
burning heart of the maiden often sighing for the
golden-headed stranger! what fears did she endure
with fainting heart! how did she often grow far paler 100
than with the gleam of gold, when desiring to contend with the savage monster Theseus was setting
forth to win either death or the meed of valour.
Yet not unsweet were the gifts, though vainly promised to the gods, which she kindled with silent lip.
For as a tree which waves its boughs on Taurus' 105
top, an oak or a cone-bearing pine with sweating
bark, when a vehement storm twists the grain with
its blast, and tears it up;—afar, wrenched away by
the roots it lies prone, breaking in its fall all that
meets it—so did Theseus lay low the conquered 110
bulk of the savage, vainly tossing his horns to the
empty winds. Thence he retraced his way, unharmed
and with much glory, guiding his devious footsteps
by the fine clew, lest as he came forth from the
windings of the labyrinth the inextricable entangle-
ment of the building should bewilder him.   115

But why should I leave the first subject of my
song and tell of more; how the daughter, leaving her
father's face, the embrace of her sister, then of her
mother last, who lamented, undone by grief for her
daughter, chose before all these the sweet love of 120
Theseus; or how the ship was borne to the foaming
shores of Dia; or how when her eyes were bound
with soft sleep her spouse left her, departing with
forgetful breast? Often in the madness of her burning

clarisonas imo fudisse e pectore voces,   125
ac tum praeruptos tristem conscendere montes,
unde aciem in pelagi vastos protenderet aestus,
tum tremuli salis adversas procurrere in undas
mollia nudatae tollentem tegmina surae,
atque haec extremis maestam dixisse querellis,   130
frigidulos udo singultus ore cientem.
  'Sicine me patriis avectam, perfide, ab aris,
perfide, deserto liquisti in litore, Theseu?
sicine discedens neglecto numine divum
immemor a, devota domum periuria portas?   135
nullane res potuit crudelis flectere mentis
consilium? tibi nulla fuit clementia praesto,
immite ut nostri vellet miserescere pectus?
at non haec quondam blanda promissa dedisti
voce mihi; non haec miseram sperare iubebas,   140
sed conubia laeta, sed optatos hymenaeos:
quae cuncta aerii discerpunt irrita venti.
iam iam nulla viro iuranti femina credat,
nulla viri speret sermones esse fideles;
quis dum aliquid cupiens animus praegestit apisci, 145
nil metuunt iurare, nihil promittere parcunt:
sed simul ac cupidae mentis satiata libidost,
dicta nihil metuere, nihil periuria curant.
certe ego te in medio versantem turbine leti
eripui, et potius germanum amittere crevi,   150
quam tibi fallaci supremo in tempore deessem;
pro quo dilaceranda feris dabor alitibusque
praeda, neque iniacta tumulabor mortua terra.
quaenam te genuit sola sub rupe leaena?
quod mare conceptum spumantibus expuit undis, 155

heart they say that she uttered piercing cries from 125
her inmost breast; and now would she sadly climb
the rugged mountains, thence to strain her eyes
over the waste of ocean-tide; now run out to
meet the waters of the rippling brine, lifting the
soft vesture of her bared knee. And thus said she 130
mournfully in her last laments, uttering cold sobs
with tearful face:—

'Thus then, having borne me afar from my father's
'home, faithless lover, thus hast thou left me, faith-
'less Theseus, on the lonely shore? thus departing,
'unmindful of the will of the gods, forgetful, ah! dost 135
'thou carry to thy home the curse of perjury? could
'nothing bend the purpose of thy cruel mind? was
'no mercy present in thy soul, to bid thy ruthless
'heart incline to pity for me? Not such were the
'promises thou gavest me once with winning voice, 140
'not this didst thou bid me hope, ah me! no, but
'a joyful wedlock, but a desired espousal; all which
'at once the winds of heaven blow abroad in vain.
'Henceforth let no woman believe a man's oath, let
'none believe that a man's speeches can be trust-
'worthy. They, while their mind desires something 145
'and longs eagerly to gain it, nothing fear to swear,
'nothing spare to promise; but as soon as the lust
'of their greedy mind is satisfied, they fear not then
'their words, they heed not their perjuries. I—thou
'knowest it—when thou wert tossing in the very whirl
'of death, saved thee, and set my heart rather to let 150
'my brother go than to fail thee, now so faithless
'found, in thy utmost need. And for this I shall be
'given to beasts and birds to tear as a prey; my corpse
'shall have no sepulture, be sprinkled with no earth.
'What lioness bore thee under a desert rock? what
'sea conceived thee and vomited thee forth from his 155

quae Syrtis, quae Scylla rapax, quae vasta Cha-
     rybdis,
talia qui reddis pro dulci praemia vita?
si tibi non cordi fuerant conubia nostra,
saeva quod horrebas prisci praecepta parentis,
at tamen in vostras potuisti ducere sedes,   160
quae tibi iucundo famularer serva labore,
candida permulcens liquidis vestigia lymphis
purpureave tuum consternens veste cubile.
sed quid ego ignaris nequiquam conquerar auris,
externata malo, quae nullis sensibus auctae   165
nec missas audire queunt nec reddere voces?
ille autem prope iam mediis versatur in undis,
nec quisquam apparet vacua mortalis in alga.
sic nimis insultans extremo tempore saeva
fors etiam nostris invidit questibus aures.   170
Iuppiter omnipotens, utinam ne tempore primo
Gnosia Cecropiae tetigissent litora puppes,
indomito nec dira ferens stipendia tauro
perfidus in Cretam religasset navita funem,
nec malus hic celans dulci crudelia forma   175
consilia in nostris requiesset sedibus hospes!
nam quo me referam? quali spe perdita nitor?
*Idomeneosne petam montes? a, gurgite lato
discernens ponti truculentum †ubi dividit aequor?
an patris auxilium sperem? quemne ipsa reliqui, 180
respersum iuvenem fraterna caede secuta?
coniugis an fido consoler memet amore,
quine fugit lentos incurvans gurgite remos?
praeterea nullo litus, sola insula, tecto,
nec patet egressus pelagi cingentibus undis: 185
nulla fugae ratio, nulla spes: omnia muta,
omnia sunt deserta, ostentant omnia letum.

'foaming waves? what Syrtis, what ravening Scylla,
'what waste Charybdis bore thee, who for sweet life
'returnest such meed as this? Though marriage with
'me had not been dear to thee for dread of the harsh
'bidding of thy stern father, yet thou couldst have 160
'led me into thy dwellings to serve thee as a slave
'with labour of love, laving thy white feet with liquid
'water, or with purple coverlet spreading thy bed.
'But why should I cry in vain to the senseless airs
'distracted with woe,—the airs that are endowed 165
'with no feeling, and can neither hear nor return
'the messages of my voice? He meanwhile is now
'tossing almost in mid-sea, and no human being is
'seen on the waste and weedy shore. Thus over-
'weening fortune too in this supreme hour has cruelly 170
'grudged her ears to my complaints. Almighty
'Jupiter, O that never once the Attic ships had
'touched Gnosian shores, nor bearing the dreadful
'tribute to the savage bull the faithless sailor had
'unmoored his cable for Crete, nor that this evil man, 175
'hiding cruel designs under a fair outside, had reposed
'in our dwellings as a guest! For whither shall I re-
'turn, lost, ah lost? on what hope do I lean? shall I
'seek the mountains of Idomeneus?—how broad the
'flood, how savage the tract of sea which divides
'them from me! Shall I hope for the aid of my 180
'father?—whom I deserted of my own will, to
'follow a lover dabbled with my brother's blood?
'Or shall I console myself with the faithful love of
'my spouse, who is flying from me, bending his
'tough oars in the wave? and here too is but the
'shore, with never a house, a desert island; no way
'to depart opens for me; about me are the waters of 185
'the sea, no means of flight, no hope; all is dumb,
'all is desolate; all shows me the face of death. Yet

non tamen ante mihi languescent lumina morte,
nec prius a fesso secedent corpore sensus,
quam iustam a divis exposcam prodita multam, 190
caelestumque fidem postrema comprecer hora.
quare facta virum multantes vindice poena,
Eumenides, quibus anguino redimita capillo
frons expirantes praeportat pectoris iras,
huc huc adventate, meas audite querellas,   195
quas ego, vae, misera extremis proferre medullis
cogor inops, ardens, amenti caeca furore.
quae quoniam verae nascuntur pectore ab imo,
vos nolite pati nostrum vanescere luctum ;
sed quali solam Theseus me mente reliquit,   200
tali mente, deae, funestet seque suosque.'
    Has postquam maesto profudit pectore voces,
supplicium saevis exposcens anxia factis,
annuit invicto caelestum numine rector,
quo *motu tellus atque horrida contremuerunt   205
aequora concussitque micantia sidera mundus.
ipse autem caeca mentem caligine Theseus
consitus oblito dimisit pectore cuncta,
quae mandata prius constanti mente tenebat,
dulcia nec maesto sustollens signa parenti   210
sospitem Erechtheum se ostendit visere portum.
namque ferunt olim, †classi cum moenia divae
linquentem gnatum ventis concrederet Aegeus,
talia complexum iuveni mandata dedisse.
'gnate mihi longa iucundior unice vita,   215
reddite in extrema nuper mihi fine senectae,   217
gnate, ego quem in dubios cogor dimittere casus, 216
quandoquidem fortuna mea ac tua fervida virtus

'my eyes shall not grow faint in death, nor shall the
'sense fail from my wearied body, before I demand
'from the gods just vengeance for my betrayal, and 190
'call upon the faith of the heavenly ones in my last
'hour. Therefore, O ye that visit the deeds of men
'with vengeful pains, ye Eumenides, whose foreheads
'bound with snaky hair bear on their front the
'wrath which breathes from your breast, hither,
'hither haste, hear my complaints which I (ah, 195
'unhappy!) utter from my inmost heart perforce,
'helpless, burning, blinded with raging frenzy. For
'since my woes come truthfully from the depths
'of my heart, suffer not ye my grief to come to
'nothing: but even as Theseus left me desolate, 200
'so, goddesses, may he bring ruin on himself and
'his own!'

When she had poured forth these words from
her sad breast, earnestly demanding vengeance for
cruel deeds; the Lord of the heavenly ones bowed
assent with sovereign nod, and with that gesture 205
trembled the earth and stormy seas, and the heavens
shook the quivering stars. But Theseus himself,
darkling in his thoughts with blind dimness, let slip
from his forgetful mind all the biddings which
formerly he had held firm with constant heart, and
raised not the welcome sign to his mourning father, 210
nor showed that he was safely sighting the Erechthean
harbour. For they say that erewhile, when Aegeus
was trusting his son to the winds, as with his fleet
he left the walls of the goddess, he embraced the
youth and gave him this charge: 'My son, my only 215
'son, dearer to me than all my length of days, re-
'stored to me but now in the last end of old age, 217
'my son, whom I perforce let go forth to doubtful 216
'hazards,—since my fortune and thy burning valour

eripit invito mihi te, cui languida nondum
lumina sunt gnati cara saturata figura :   220
non ego te gaudens laetanti pectore mittam,
nec te ferre sinam fortunae signa secundae,
sed primum multas expromam mente querellas,
canitiem terra atque infuso pulvere foedans;
inde infecta vago suspendam lintea malo,   225
nostros ut luctus nostraeque incendia mentis
carbasus obscurata †dicet ferrugine Hibera.
quod tibi si sancti concesserit incola Itoni,
quae nostrum genus ac sedes defendere Erechthei
annuit, ut tauri respergas sanguine dextram,   230
tum vero facito ut memori tibi condita corde
haec vigeant mandata, nec ulla oblitteret aetas,
ut simul ac nostros invisent lumina collis,
funestam antennae deponant undique vestem,
candidaque intorti sustollant vela rudentes,   235
quam primum cernens ut laeta gaudia mente
agnoscam, cum te reducem aetas prospera sistet.'
   Haec mandata prius constanti mente tenentem
Thesea ceu pulsae ventorum flamine nubes
aerium nivei montis liquere cacumen.   240
at pater, ut summa prospectum ex arce petebat,
anxia in assiduos absumens lumina fletus,
cum primum inflati conspexit lintea veli,
praecipitem sese scopulorum e vertice iecit,
amissum credens immiti Thesea fato.   245
sic funesta domus ingressus tecta paterna
morte ferox Theseus qualem Minoidi luctum
obtulerat mente immemori talem ipse recepit.

'tears thee from me, unwilling me, whose failing
'eyes are not yet satisfied with the dear image 220
'of my son, I will not let thee go gladly with
'cheerful heart, nor suffer thee to bear the tokens of
'prosperous fortune: but first will bring forth many
'laments from my heart, soiling my gray hairs with
'earth and showered dust: thereafter will I hang 225
'dyed sails on thy roving mast, that so the tale of
'my grief and the fire that burns in my heart may
'be marked by the canvas stained with Iberian
'azure. But if she who dwells in holy Itonus, who
'vouchsafes to defend our race and the abodes of
'Erechtheus, shall grant thee to sprinkle thy right 230
'hand with the bull's blood, then be sure that these
'biddings live, laid up in thy mindful heart, and
'that no length of time blur them: that as soon as
'thy eyes shall come within sight of our hills, thy
'yardarms may lay down from them their mourning
'raiment, and the twisted cordage raise a white sail: 235
'that so I may see at once and gladly welcome the
'signs of joy, when a happy hour shall set thee here
'in thy home again.'

These biddings at first did Theseus preserve
with constant mind; but then they left him, as
clouds driven by the blast of the winds leave the 240
lofty head of the snowy mountain. But the father,
as he gazed out from his tower top, wasting his
eyes care-worn in constant tear-floods, when first he
saw the canvas of the bellying sail, threw himself
headlong from the summit of the rocks, believing 245
Theseus destroyed by ruthless fate. Thus bold
Theseus, as he entered the chambers of his home,
darkened with mourning for his father's death, himself received such grief as by forgetfulness of heart
he had caused to the daughter of Minos. And she

quae tamen aspectans cedentem maesta carinam
multiplices animo volvebat saucia curas.   250
    At parte ex alia florens volitabat Iacchus
cum thiaso Satyrorum et Nysigenis Silenis,
te quaerens, Ariadna, tuoque incensus amore.
qui tum alacres passim lymphata mente furebant
euhoe bacchantes, euhoe capita inflectentes.   255

          *   *   *   *

harum pars tecta quatiebant cuspide thyrsos,
pars e divulso iactabant membra iuvenco,
pars sese tortis serpentibus incingebant,
pars obscura cavis celebrabant orgia cistis,
orgia, quae frustra cupiunt audire profani;   260
plangebant aliae proceris tympana palmis
aut tereti tenues tinnitus aere ciebant,
multis raucisonos efflabant cornua bombos
barbaraque horribili stridebat tibia cantu.

    Talibus amplifice vestis decorata figuris   265
pulvinar complexa suo velabat amictu.
quae postquam cupide spectando Thessala pubes
expletast, sanctis coepit decedere divis.
hic, qualis flatu placidum mare matutino
horrificans Zephyrus proclivas incitat undas   270
Aurora exoriente vagi sub limina Solis,
quae tarde primum clementi flamine pulsae
procedunt, leviterque sonant plangore cachinni,
post vento crescente magis magis increbescunt
purpureaque procul nantes ab luce refulgent,   275
sic ibi vestibuli linquentes regia tecta
ad se quisque vago passim pede discedebant.

the while, gazing tearfully at the retreating ship, was 250
revolving manifold cares in her wounded heart.

In another part of the tapestry youthful Bacchus
was wandering with the rout of Satyrs and the Nysa-
born Sileni, seeking thee, Ariadna, and fired with thy
love ; who then, busy here and there, were raging with
frenzied mind, Evoe! crying tumultuously, Evoe! 255
shaking their heads.

       *   *   *   *

Some of them were waving thyrsi with shrouded
points, some tossing about the limbs of a mangled
steer, some girding themselves with writhing serpents:
some bearing solemnly dark mysteries enclosed in
caskets, mysteries which the profane desire in vain 260
to hear. Others beat timbrels with uplifted hands,
or raised clear clashings with cymbals of rounded
bronze : many blew horns with harsh-sounding drone,
and the barbarian pipe shrilled with dreadful din.

Such were the figures that richly adorned the 265
tapestry which embraced and shrouded with its folds
the royal couch. Now when the Thessalian youth
had gazed their fill, fixing their eager eyes on these
wonders, they began to give place to the holy gods.
Hereupon, as the west wind ruffling the quiet sea with 270
its breath at morn urges on the sloping waves, when
the Dawn is rising up to the gates of the travelling
sun, the waters slowly at first, driven by gentle breeze
step on and lightly sound with plash of laughter;
then as the breeze grows fresh they crowd on close
and closer, and floating afar reflect a brightness
from the crimson light ; so now, leaving the royal 275
buildings of the portal, hither and thither variously
with devious feet the guests passed away. After

quorum post abitum princeps e vertice Peli
advenit Chiron portans silvestria dona;
nam quoscumque ferunt campi, quos Thessala mag-
　　　nis　　　　　　　　　　　　　　　　　　　280
montibus ora creat, quos propter fluminis undas
aura aperit flores tepidi fecunda Favoni,
hos indistinctis plexos tulit ipse corollis,
quo permulsa domus iucundo risit odore.
confestim Penios adest, viridantia Tempe,　　285
Tempe, quae silvae cingunt super impendentes,
†Minosim linquens †Doris celebranda choreis,
non vacuus: namque ille tulit radicitus altas
fagos ac recto proceras stipite laurus,
non sine nutanti platano lentaque sorore　　290
flammati Phaethontis et aeria cupressu.
haec circum sedes late contexta locavit,
vestibulum ut molli velatum fronde vireret.
post hunc consequitur sollerti corde Prometheus,
extenuata gerens veteris vestigia poenae,　　295
quam quondam †silici restrictus membra catena
persolvit pendens e verticibus praeruptis.
inde pater divum sancta cum coniuge natisque
advenit caelo te solum, Phoebe, relinquens
unigenamque simul cultricem montibus †Idri:　300
Pelea nam tecum pariter soror aspernatast
nec Thetidis taedas voluit celebrare iugalis.
qui postquam niveis flexerunt sedibus artus,
large multiplici constructae sunt dape mensae,
cum interea infirmo quatientes corpora motu　305
veridicos Parcae coeperunt edere cantus.
his corpus tremulum complectens undique vestis
candida purpurea *talos incinxerat ora,
at roseae niveo residebant vertice vittae,
aeternumque manus carpebant rite laborem.　310

their departure, from the top of Pelion came Chiron
leading the way, bearing woodland gifts. For all the
flowers that the plains bear, all that the Thessalian 280
region brings to birth on its mighty mountains, all
the flowers that near the river's streams the fruitful
gale of warm Favonius discloses, these he brought
himself, woven in mingled garlands, cheered with
which the house smiled with grateful odour. Forth-
with Peneus is there, leaving verdant Tempe, Tempe 285
girt with impendent forests   to be haunted by
Dorian dances; not empty-handed; for he bore,
torn up by the roots, lofty beeches and tall bay trees
with straight stem, and with them the nodding plane 290
and the swaying sister of flame-devoured Phaethon,
and the tall cypress. All these he wove far and
wide around their home, that the portal might be
greenly embowered with soft foliage. Next follows
him Prometheus wise of heart, bearing the faded 295
scars of the ancient penalty which whilom, his limbs
bound fast to the rock with chains, he paid, hanging
from the craggy summits. Then came the Father of
the Gods with his divine wife and his sons, leaving
thee, Phoebus, alone in heaven, and with thee thine 300
own sister who dwells in the mountains of Idrus;
for as thou didst, so did thy sister scorn Peleus,
nor deigned to be present at the nuptial torches of
Thetis.

So when they had bent their limbs on the white
seats, bountifully were the tables piled with varied 305
dainties: whilst in the meantime, swaying their
bodies with palsied motion, the Parcae began to
utter soothtelling chants. White raiment enfolding
their aged forms robed their ankles with a crimson
border; on their snowy heads rested rosy bands,
while their hands duly plied the eternal task. The 310

laeva colum molli lana retinebat amictum,
dextera tum leviter deducens fila supinis
formabat digitis, tum prono in pollice torquens
libratum tereti versabat turbine fusum,
atque ita decerpens aequabat semper opus dens, 315
laneaque aridulis haerebant morsa labellis,
quae prius in levi fuerant extantia filo:
ante pedes autem candentis mollia lanae
vellera virgati custodibant calathisci.
haec tum clarisona pellentes vellera voce   320
talia divino fuderunt carmine fata,
carmine, perfidiae quod post nulla arguet aetas.

O decus eximium magnis virtutibus augens,
Emathiae tutamen opis, clarissime nato,
accipe, quod laeta tibi pandunt luce sorores,   325
veridicum oraclum. sed vos, quae fata sequuntur,
    currite ducentes subtegmina, currite, fusi.

adveniet tibi iam portans optata maritis
Hesperus, adveniet fausto cum sidere coniunx,
quae tibi †flexo animo mentis perfundet amorem† 330
languidulosque paret tecum coniungere somnos,
levia substernens robusto bracchia collo.
    currite ducentes subtegmina, currite, fusi.

nulla domus tales umquam contexit amores,
nullus amor tali coniunxit foedere amantes,   335
qualis adest Thetidi, qualis concordia Peleo.
    currite ducentes subtegmina, currite, fusi.

nascetur vobis expers terroris Achilles,
hostibus haud tergo, sed forti pectore notus,
qui persaepe vago victor certamine cursus   340
flammea praevertet celeris vestigia cervae.
    currite ducentes subtegmina, currite, fusi.

left hand held the distaff clothed with soft wool;
then the right hand lightly drawing out the threads
with upturned fingers shaped them, then with downward thumb twirled the spindle poised with rounded 315
whorl; and so with their teeth they still plucked the
threads and made the work even. Bitten ends of
wool clung to their dry lips, which had before stood
out from the smooth yarn: and at their feet soft
fleeces of white-shining wool were kept safe in bas-
kets of osier. They then, as they struck the wool, 320
sang with clear voice, and thus poured forth the fates
in divine chant, chant, which no length of time shall
prove untruthful.

'O thou who crownest high renown with great
'deeds of virtue, bulwark of Emathian power, famed
'for thy son to be, receive the soothtelling oracle 325
'which on this happy day the Sisters reveal to thee;
'but do ye run, drawing the woof-threads which the
'fates follow, ye spindles, run.

'Soon will Hesperus come to thee, Hesperus, who
'brings longed-for gifts to the wedded, will come with
'happy star thy wife, to shed over thy spirit soul- 330
'quelling love, and join with thee restful slumbers,
'laying her smooth arms under thy strong neck.
'Run, drawing the woof-threads, ye spindles, run.

'No house ever covered such loves as these; no
'love ever joined lovers in such a bond as links 335
'Thetis and Peleus, heart in heart. Run, drawing
'the woof-threads, ye spindles, run.

'There shall be born to you a son that knows
'not fear, Achilles, known to his enemies not by his
'back but by his stout breast; who right often 340
'winner in the contest of the wide-ranging race shall
'outstrip the flame-fleet footsteps of the flying hind.
'Run, drawing the woof-threads, ye spindles, run.

non illi quisquam bello se conferet heros,
cum Phrygii Teucro manabunt sanguine *rivi,
Troicaque obsidens longinquo moenia bello   345
periuri Pelopis vastabit tertius heres.
    currite ducentes subtegmina, currite, fusi.

illius egregias virtutes claraque facta
saepe fatebuntur gnatorum in funere matres,
cum *incultum cano* solvent a vertice crinem   350
putridaque infirmis variabunt pectora palmis.
    currite ducentes subtegmina, currite, fusi.

namque velut densas praecerpens cultor aristas
sole sub ardenti flaventia demetit arva,
Troiugenum infesto prosternet corpora ferro.   355
    currite ducentes subtegmina, currite, fusi.

testis erit magnis virtutibus unda Scamandri,
quae passim rapido diffunditur Hellesponto,
cuius iter caesis angustans corporum acervis
alta tepefaciet permixta flumina caede.   360
    currite ducentes subtegmina, currite, fusi.

    *   *   *   *

denique testis erit morti quoque reddita praeda,
cum teres excelso coacervatum aggere bustum
excipiet niveos percussae virginis artus.
    currite ducentes subtegmina, currite, fusi.   365

nam simul ac fessis dederit fors copiam Achivis
urbis Dardaniae Neptunia solvere vincla,
alta Polyxenia madefient caede sepulcra,
quae, velut ancipiti succumbens victima ferro,

'Against him not a hero shall match himself in
'war, when the Phrygian streams shall flow with
'Teucrian blood, and the Trojan walls, with tedious 345
'war beleaguering, the third heir of Pelops shall
'lay waste.   Run, drawing the woof-threads, ye
'spindles, run.

'The hero's surpassing achievements and re-
'nowned deeds often shall mothers own at the
'burial of their sons, loosing dishevelled hair from 350
'hoary head, and marring their withered breasts with
'weak hands.   Run, drawing the woof-threads, ye
'spindles, run.

'For as the husbandman cropping the thick ears
'of corn under the burning sun mows down the
'yellow fields, so shall he lay low with foeman's 355
'steel the bodies of the sons of Troy.   Run, drawing
'the woof-threads, ye spindles, run.

'Witness of his great deeds of valour shall be
'the wave of Scamander which pours itself forth
'abroad in the current of Hellespont, whose channel
'with heaps of slain corpses he shall choke, and make
'the deep streams warm with mingled blood.   Run, 360
'drawing the woof-threads, ye spindles, run.

*   *   *   *

'Lastly, witness too shall be the prize assigned
'to him in death, when the rounded barrow heaped
'up with lofty mound shall receive the snowy limbs
'of the slaughtered maiden.   Run, drawing the woof- 365
'threads, ye spindles, run.

'For so soon as fortune shall give to the weary
'Achaeans power to loose the Neptune-forged circlet
'of the Dardanian town, the high tomb shall be
'wetted with Polyxena's blood, who like a victim
'falling under the two-edged steel, shall bend her

proiciet truncum submisso poplite corpus.   370
    currite ducentes subtegmina, currite, fusi.

quare agite optatos animi coniungite amores.
accipiat coniunx felici foedere divam,
dedatur cupido iamdudum nupta marito.
    currite ducentes subtegmina, currite, fusi.   375

     .   .   .   .

anxia nec mater discordis maesta puellae
secubitu caros mittet sperare nepotes.   380
    currite ducentes subtegmina, currite, fusi.

Talia praefantes quondam felicia † Pelei
carmina divino cecinere * e pectore Parcae.
praesentes namque ante domos invisere castas
heroum et sese mortali ostendere coetu   385
caelicolae nondum spreta pietate solebant.
saepe pater divum templo in fulgente revisens
annua cum festis venissent sacra diebus,
conspexit terra centum procumbere tauros.
saepe vagus Liber Parnasi vertice summo   390
Thyadas effusis euantis crinibus egit,
cum Delphi tota certatim ex urbe ruentes
acciperent laeti divum fumantibus aris.
saepe in letifero belli certamine Mavors
aut rapidi Tritonis era aut Rhamnusia virgo   395
armatas hominumst praesens hortata catervas.
sed postquam tellus scelerest imbuta nefando,
iustitiamque omnes cupida de mente fugarunt,
perfudere manus fraterno sanguine fratres,
destitit extinctos natus lugere parentes,   400
optavit genitor primaevi funera nati,
liber ut innuptae poteretur flore novercae,
ignaro mater substernens se impia nato

'knee and bow her headless trunk. Run, drawing 370
'the woof-threads, ye spindles, run.

   'Come then, unite the loves which your souls
'desire: let the husband receive in happy bonds the
'goddess, let the bride be given up—nay now!—
'to her eager spouse. Run, drawing the woof- 375
'threads, ye spindles, run.

.   .   .   .

   'Nor shall her anxious mother, saddened by lone- 380
'lying of an unkindly bride, give up the hope of
'dear descendants. Run, drawing the woof-threads,
'ye spindles, run.'
   Such strains of divination in days of yore, fore-
boding happiness to Peleus, sang the Fates from
prophetic breast. For in bodily presence of old, before
religion was despised, the heavenly ones were wont to 385
visit pious homes of heroes, and show themselves to
mortal company. Often the Father of the gods coming
down again, in his bright temple, when yearly feasts
had come on holy days, saw a hundred bulls fall to
the ground. Often Liber roving on the topmost height 390
of Parnassus drove the Thyades crying Evoe with
flying hair, when the Delphians, racing eagerly from
all the town, joyfully received the god with smoking
altars. Often in the death-bearing strife of war
Mavors or the Lady of swift Triton or the Rhamnu- 395
sian Maid by their presence stirred up the courage
of armed bands of men. But when the earth was
dyed with hideous crime, and all men banished
justice from their greedy souls, and brothers dipped
their hands in brothers' blood, the son left off to 400
mourn his parents' death, the father wished for
the death of his young son, that he might without
hindrance enjoy the flower of a young bride, the

impia non veritast divos scelerare parentes:
omnia fanda nefanda malo permixta furore   405
iustificam nobis mentem avertere deorum.
quare nec tales dignantur visere coetus,
nec se contingi patiuntur lumine claro.

LXV

Etsi me assiduo confectum cura dolore
    sevocat a doctis, Hortale, virginibus,
nec potis est dulcis Musarum expromere fetus
    mens animi, tantis fluctuat ipsa malis:
namque mei nuper Lethaeo gurgite fratris   5
    pallidulum manans alluit unda pedem,
Troia Rhoeteo quem subter litore tellus
    ereptum nostris obterit ex oculis.

    *   *   *   *

[alloquar, audiero numquam tua [facta] loquentem,]
    numquam ego te, vita frater amabilior,   10
aspiciam posthac. at certe semper amabo,
    semper maesta tua carmina morte *canam,
qualia sub densis ramorum concinit umbris
    Daulias absumpti fata gemens Ityli—
sed tamen in tantis maeroribus, Hortale, mitto   15
    haec expressa tibi carmina Battiadae,
ne tua dicta vagis nequiquam credita ventis
    effluxisse meo forte putes animo,
ut missum sponsi furtivo munere malum
    procurrit casto virginis e gremio,   20
quod miserae oblitae molli sub veste locatum,
    dum adventu matris prosilit, excutitur:
atque illud prono praeceps agitur decursu,
    huic manat tristi conscius ore rubor.

unnatural mother coupling with her unconscious son did not fear to sin against parental gods: then all right and wrong, confounded in impious madness, 405 turned from us the righteous will of the gods. Wherefore they deign not to visit such companies, nor endure the touch of clear daylight.

LXV

To Hortalus.

Though I am worn out with constant grief, Hortalus, and sorrow calls me apart from the learned Maids, nor can the thoughts of my heart utter the sweet births of the Muses, tossed as it is with such waves of trouble;—so lately the 5 creeping wave of the Lethaean flood laps my own brother's death-pale foot, on whom, torn away from our sight, the Trojan earth under the shore of Rhoeteum lies heavy. Never shall I speak to thee, never hear thee tell of thy life; never shall I see 10 thee again, brother more beloved than life. But surely I will always love thee, always sing strains of mourning for thy death, as under the thick shadows of the boughs sings the Daulian bird be- wailing the fate of Itylus lost. Yet, in such sorrows, 15 Hortalus, I send to you these verses of Battiades translated, lest haply you should think that your words vainly committed to wandering winds have slipped from my mind: as an apple sent as a secret gift from her betrothed lover falls out from the 20 chaste bosom of the girl, which—poor child, she forgot it!—put away in her soft gown, is shaken out as she starts forward when her mother comes; then, see, onward, downward swiftly it rolls and runs; a conscious blush creeps over her downcast face.

LXVI

Omnia qui magni dispexit lumina mundi,
   qui stellarum ortus comperit atque obitus,
flammeus ut rapidi solis nitor obscuretur,
   ut cedant certis sidera temporibus,
ut Triviam furtim sub Latmia saxa relegans   5
   dulcis amor gyro devocet aerio,
idem me ille Conon caelesti in lumine vidit
   e Beroniceo vertice caesariem
fulgentem clare, quam †multis illa dearum†
   levia portendens bracchia pollicitast,   10
qua rex tempestate novo auctus hymenaeo
   vastatum finis iverat Assyrios.

estne novis nuptis odio Venus †atque parentum† 15
   frustrantur falsis gaudia lacrimulis,
ubertim thalami quas intra limina fundunt?
   non, ita me divi, vera gemunt, iuerint.
id mea me multis docuit regina querellis
   invisente novo praelia torva viro.   20
at tu non orbum luxti deserta cubile,
   sed fratris cari flebile discidium,
cum penitus maestas exedit cura medullas!
   ut tibi tum toto pectore sollicitae
sensibus ereptis mens excidit! at te ego certe 25
   cognoram a parva virgine magnanimam.
anne bonum oblita's facinus, quo regium adepta's
   coniugium, quo non fortius ausit alis?
sed tum maesta virum mittens quae verba locuta's!
   Iuppiter, ut tristi lumina saepe manu!   30

LXVI

The Lock of Berenice.

Conon, he who surveyed all the lights of the
great heaven, who learnt the risings of the stars and
their settings, how the flaming blaze of the swift
sun is darkened, how the stars recede at set seasons,
how sweet love calls Trivia from her airy circuit, 5
banishing her secretly to the rocky cave of Latmus
—that same Conon saw me shining brightly among
the lights of heaven, me, the lock from the head of
Berenice, me whom she vowed to many of the goddesses, stretching forth her smooth arms, at that 10
season when the king, blest in his new marriage,
had gone to waste the Assyrian borders. . . . Is
Venus hated by new brides? and do they mock the
joys of parents with false tears, which they shed 15
plentifully within the bridal chamber? No, so may
the gods help me, they lament not truly. This
my queen taught me by all her laments, when
her newly-wedded husband went forth to grim war.
But your tears, forsooth, were not shed for the 20
desertion of your widowed bed, but for the mourn-
ful parting from your dear brother, when sorrow
gnawed the inmost marrow of your sad heart. At
that time how from your whole breast did your
anxious soul fail, bereft of sense! and yet truly I 25
knew you to be stout-hearted from young girlhood.
Have you forgotten the brave deed by which you
gained a royal marriage, braver deed than which
none other could ever dare? But then in your grief,
when parting from your husband, what words did
you utter! How often, O Juppiter, did you brush 30

quis te mutavit tantus deus? an quod amantes
    non longe a caro corpore abesse volunt?
atque ibi me cunctis pro dulci coniuge divis
    non sine taurino sanguine pollicita's,
si reditum tetulisset. is haud in tempore longo   35
    captam Asiam Aegypti finibus addiderat.
quis ego pro factis caelesti reddita coetu
    pristina vota novo munere dissoluo.
invita, o regina, tuo de vertice cessi,
    invita: adiuro teque tuumque caput,   40
digna ferat quod siquis inaniter adiurarit:
    sed qui se ferro postulet esse parem?
ille quoque eversus mons est, quem maximum in
        †oris
    progenies Thiae clara supervehitur,
cum Medi peperere novum mare, cumque iuventus   45
    per medium classi barbara navit Athon.
quid facient crines, cum ferro talia cedant?
    Iuppiter, ut Chalybon omne genus pereat,
et qui principio sub terra quaerere venas
    institit ac ferri stringere duritiem!   50
abiunctae paulo ante comae mea fata sorores
    lugebant, cum se Memnonis Aethiopis
unigena impellens nutantibus aera pennis
    obtulit Arsinoes Locridos ales equus,
isque per aetherias me tollens avolat umbras   55
    et Veneris casto collocat in gremio.
ipsa suum Zephyritis eo famulum legarat,
    Graia Canopeis incola litoribus.
inde Venus vario ne solum in lumine caeli
    ex Ariadneis aurea temporibus   60
fixa corona foret, sed nos quoque fulgeremus
    devotae flavi verticis exuviae,

away the tears with your hand! What mighty god has changed you thus? is it that lovers cannot bear to be far away from the side of him they love? And there to all the gods for your dear husband's welfare you consecrated me with blood of bulls, so he should complete his return. He in no long time had 35 added conquered Asia to the territories of Egypt. This is done; and now, given as due to the host of heaven, I pay your former vows by a new offering. Unwillingly, O queen, I was parted from your head, unwillingly, I swear both by you and by your 40 head; by which if any swear vainly, let him reap a worthy recompense. But who can claim to be as strong as steel? Even that mountain was overthrown, the greatest of all in those shores which the bright son of Thia traverses, when the Medes 45 created a new sea, and when the barbarian youth swam in their fleet through mid Athos. What shall locks of hair do, when such things as this yield to steel? O, Jupiter, may all the race of the Chalybes perish, and he, who first began to seek for veins under ground, and to draw out hard bars of iron! 50 My sister locks, sundered from me just before, were mourning for my fate, when the own brother of Ethiopian Memnon appeared, striking the air with waving wings, the winged courser of Locrian Arsinoe. And he sweeping me away flies through 55 the gales of heaven and places me in the chaste bosom of Venus. On that service had the Lady of Zephyrium herself sent her own minister, the Grecian queen, sojourner in the shores of Canopus. Then Venus—that among the various lights of heaven, not 60 only from the brows of Ariadne should the golden crown be fixed, but that I too might shine, I, the

uvidulam a †fluctu cedentem ad templa deum me
   sidus in antiquis diva novum posuit:
Virginis et saevi contingens namque Leonis   65
   lumina, Callisto iuncta Lycaoniae,
vertor in occasum, tardum dux ante Booten,
   qui vix sero alto mergitur Oceano.
sed quamquam me nocte premunt vestigia divum,
   lux autem canae Tethyi restituit,   70
(pace tua fari hic liceat, Rhamnusia virgo,
   namque ego non ullo vera timore tegam,
nec si me infestis discerpent sidera dictis,
   condita quin veri pectoris evoluam):
non his tam laetor rebus, quam me afore semper, 75
   afore me a dominae vertice discrucior,
quicum ego, dum virgo quondam fuit, omnibus
      †expers
   unguentis, una milia multa bibi.
nunc vos, optato cum iunxit lumine taeda,
   non prius unanimis corpora coniugibus   80
tradite nudantes reiecta veste papillas,
   quam iucunda mihi munera libet onyx,
vester onyx, casto colitis quae iura cubili.
   sed quae se impuro dedit adulterio,
illius a, mala dona levis bibat irrita pulvis: 85
   namque ego ab indignis praemia nulla peto.
sed magis, o nuptae, semper concordia vestras
   semper amor sedes incolat assiduus.
tu vero, regina, tuens cum sidera divam
   placabis festis luminibus Venerem,   90
*unguinis expertem non siris esse tuam me,
   sed potius largis affice muneribus.
sidera cur *retinent? iterum* coma regia fiam:
   proximus Hydrochoi fulgoret Oarion!

dedicated spoil of her sunny head—me dripping from
the wave, and transported to the abodes of the gods,
me a new constellation among the ancient stars did
the goddess set; for I, touching the fires of the Virgin 65
and the raging Lion, and close by Callisto daughter
of Lycaon, move to my setting, while I point the way
before slow Bootes, who late in night scarce dips in
deep ocean.   But though at night the footsteps of the
gods press close upon me, whilst by day I am re- 70
stored to gray Tethys: under thy sufferance let me
speak this, O Virgin of Rhamnus ;—no fear shall make
me hide the truth, no, not even though the stars shall
rend me with angry words will I refrain from uttering
the secrets of a true heart—I do not so much rejoice
in this good fortune, as grieve that absent ever, absent 75
must I be from the head of my lady ; with whom of
old, whilst she was still a virgin, I, who now share no
more in any of her perfumes, with her drank many
thousands.   Now, ye maidens, since the torch has
united you with welcome light, yield not your bodies 80
to your loving spouses, baring your breasts with
vesture opened, before the onyx jar offers pleasant
gifts to me, the jar which is yours, who reverence
marriage in chaste wedlock.   But as for her who
gives herself up to foul adultery, ah! let the light 85
dust drink up her worthless gifts unratified: for I ask
no offerings from the unworthy.   But rather, O ye
brides, may concord evermore dwell in your homes,
ever abiding Love.   And you, my queen, when gazing
on the stars you propitiate Venus with festal lamps, 90
let not me your handmaid want perfumes, but rather
enrich me with bounteous gifts.   Why do the stars
keep me here?   I would fain be the queen's hair
once more; and let Orion blaze next to Aquarius.

LXVII

O dulci iucunda viro, iucunda parenti,
   salve, teque bona Iuppiter auctet ope,
ianua, quam Balbo dicunt servisse benigne
   olim, cum sedes ipse senex tenuit,
quamque ferunt rursus nato servire maligne,   5
   postquam es porrecto facta marita sene.
dic agedum nobis, quare mutata feraris
   in dominum veterem deseruisse fidem.
'non (ita Caecilio placeam, cui tradita nunc sum)
   culpa meast, quamquam dicitur esse mea,   10
nec peccatum a me quisquam pote dicere quic-
      quam:
   verum †istius populi ianua qui te facit,†
qui, quacumque aliquid reperitur non bene factum,
   ad me omnes clamant: ianua, culpa tuast.'
non istuc satis est uno te dicere verbo,   15
   sed facere ut quivis sentiat et videat.
'qui possum? nemo quaerit nec scire laborat.'
   nos volumus: nobis dicere ne dubita.

LXVII

Catullus.

Hail, house-door, once dear to a well-beloved husband and to his father, hail, and may Jupiter bless you with kindly help; you door, who once, they say, did kindly service to Balbus, when the old man himself held the house, and who since then, 5 they tell us, are doing grudging service to his son, now that the old man is dead and laid out, and you are become the door of a wedded house.

Come tell us why you are said to be changed, and to have deserted your old faithfulness to your master.

House-door.

It is not—so may I please Caecilius whose property I am now become—it is not my fault, though 10 it is said to be mine, nor can any one speak of any wrong done by me. But of course people will have it that the door does it all; they, whenever any ill deed is discovered, all cry out to me, 'house-door, the fault is yours.'

Catullus.

It is not enough for you to say that with 15 a single word, but so to do that any one may feel and see it.

House-door.

How can I? no one asks or cares to know.

Catullus.

I wish to know—do not scruple to tell me.

'primum igitur, virgo quod fertur tradita nobis,
    falsumst.   20

atqui non solum hoc se dicit cognitum habere   31
    Brixia †Chinea suppositum specula,†
flavus quam molli percurrit flumine Mella,
    Brixia Veronae mater amata meae;
sed de Postumio et Corneli narrat amore,   35
    cum quibus illa malum fecit adulterium.'
dixerit hic aliquis: 'quid? tu istaec, ianua, nosti?
    cui numquam domini limine abesse licet,
nec populum auscultare, sed hic suffixa tigillo
    tantum operire soles aut aperire domum?'   40
'saepe illam audivi furtiva voce loquentem
    solam cum ancillis haec sua flagitia,
nomine dicentem quos diximus, ut pote quae mi
    speraret nec linguam esse nec auriculam.
praeterea addebat quendam, quem dicere nolo   45
    nomine, ne tollat rubra supercilia.
longus homost, magnas cui lites intulit olim
    falsum mendaci ventre puerperium.'

LXVIII

Quod mihi fortuna casuque oppressus acerbo
    conscriptum hoc lacrimis mittis epistolium,
naufragum ut eiectum spumantibus aequoris undis
    sublevem et a mortis limine restituam,
quem neque sancta Venus molli requiescere somno   5
    desertum in lecto caelibe perpetitur,

House-door.

First then, that she came to us a virgin is untrue. ₂₀

And yet this not only does Brixia say she well ₃₁ knows, Brixia that lies close under the citadel of Chinea, the town through which runs the soft stream of yellow Mella, Brixia dear mother of my own Verona; but she tells also of Postumius, and the amours of Cornelius, with whom she enjoyed un- ₃₅ lawful love.

Catullus.

Here someone will say: 'What, house-door, do you know all this, you who never may be away from your master's threshold, nor hear the people talk, but fixed under this lintel do nothing, but shut or open the house?' ₄₀

House-door.

I have often heard her telling these sins of hers with hushed voice alone with her maids, speaking of those by name of whom I spoke, hoping no doubt that I had neither tongue nor ear. She added besides one whom I do not choose to mention by name, lest ₄₅ he should arch his red brows. He is a tall man, and was once troubled with a great lawsuit, from a falsely imputed child-birth.

LXVIII

To Manlius.

That you, weighed down as you are by fortune and bitter chance, should send me this letter written with tears, to bid me succour a shipwrecked man cast up by the foaming waters of the sea, and restore him from the threshold of death, whom neither does ₅ holy Venus suffer to rest, deserted in his widowed

nec veterum dulci scriptorum carmine Musae
    oblectant, cum mens anxia pervigilat;
id gratumst mihi, me quoniam tibi dicis amicum,
    muneraque et Musarum hinc petis et Veneris: 10
sed tibi ne mea sint ignota incommoda, Manli,
    neu me odisse putes hospitis officium,
accipe, quis merser fortunae fluctibus ipse,
    ne amplius a misero dona beata petas.
tempore quo primum vestis mihi tradita purast, 15
    iucundum cum aetas florida ver ageret,
multa satis lusi: non est dea nescia nostri,
    quae dulcem curis miscet amaritiem:
sed totum hoc studium luctu fraterna mihi mors
    abstulit. o misero frater adempte mihi,   20
tu mea tu moriens fregisti commoda, frater,
    tecum una totast nostra sepulta domus,
omnia tecum una perierunt gaudia nostra,
    quae tuus in vita dulcis alebat amor.
cuius ego interitu tota de mente fugavi   25
    haec studia atque omnes delicias animi.
quare, quod scribis 'Veronae turpe, Catulle,
    esse, quod hic quisquis de meliore notast
frigida deserto tepefecit membra cubili,'
    id, Manli, non est turpe, magis miserumst.   30
ignosces igitur, si, quae mihi luctus ademit,
    haec tibi non tribuo munera, cum nequeo.
nam, quod scriptorum non magnast copia apud me,
    hoc fit, quod Romae vivimus: illa domus,

bed, nor do the Muses with the sweet poetry of
ancient writers charm him, when his mind keeps
anxious vigil;—this is grateful to me, since you
count me as your friend, and come to me for the 10
gifts both of the Muses and of Love.

But, dear Manlius, that my troubles may not be
unknown to you, and that you may not think I am
tired of the duty of a friend, let me tell you what
are the waves of fortune in which I too am whelmed;
so will you not again require gifts of happiness from
one who is unblest.

At the time when first a white dress was given 15
to me, when my youth in its flower was keeping
jocund spring time, I wrote merry poems enough;
not unacquainted with me is the goddess who mingles
with her cares a sweet bitterness.

But all care for this is gone from me by my
brother's death. Ah me unhappy, who have lost 20
you, my brother! You, brother, you by your
death have destroyed my happiness; with you all
my house is buried. With you all my joys have
perished, which your sweet love cherished, while you
yet lived. By reason of your death, I have banished 25
from all my mind these thoughts and all the pleasures
of my heart.

And so, when you write 'It is no credit to you,
Catullus, to be at Verona; because here, where
I am, all the young men of better condition warm
their cold limbs in the bed deserted by you'; that, 30
Manlius, is rather a sorrow than a discredit. You
will forgive me then, if I do not render to you
those services which grief has taken from me, since
I cannot do it.

For as for my not having plenty of authors at
hand, that is because I live at Rome: that is my

illa mihi sedes, illic mea carpitur aetas: 35
   huc una ex multis capsula me sequitur.
quod cum ita sit, nolim statuas nos mente maligna
   id facere aut animo non satis ingenuo,
quod tibi non utriusque petenti copia praestost:
   ultro ego deferrem, copia siqua foret.   40

LXVIII a

non possum reticere, deae, qua me Allius in re
   iuverit aut quantis iuverit officiis:
ne fugiens saeclis obliviscentibus aetas
   illius hoc caeca nocte tegat studium:
45 sed dicam vobis, vos porro dicite multis   5
   milibus et facite haec charta loquatur anus

     *   *   *   *

   notescatque magis mortuus atque magis,
nec tenuem texens sublimis aranea telam
50   in deserto Alli nomine opus faciat.   10
nam mihi quam dederit duplex Amathusia curam,
   scitis, et in quo me corruerit genere,
cum tantum arderem quantum Trinacria rupes
   lymphaque in Oetaeis Malia Thermopylis,
55 maesta neque assiduo tabescere lumina fletu   15
   cessarent tristique imbre madere genae.
qualis in aerii perlucens vertice montis
   rivus muscoso prosilit e lapide,
qui cum de prona praeceps est valle volutus,
60   per medium densi transit iter populi,   20
dulce viatori lasso in sudore levamen,
   cum gravis exustos aestus hiulcat agros:

home, that is my abode, there my life is spent; when 35
I come here only one box out of many follows me.
And since this is so, I would not have you judge that
it is due to niggardly mind or ungenerous temper,
that you have not received a full supply of what you
ask of each kind: I would have offered it unasked, if 40
I had any such resources.

LXVIII a

I cannot, ye goddesses, be silent about the matter
in which Allius helped me, and how greatly he helped
me by his services, lest time flying with forgetful ages
45 hide this zeal of his in blind night. But I will tell 5
you; do you hand on the tale to many thousands,
and let the paper speak this in its old age.

*   *   *   *

and let him be famous more and more in death;
and let not the spider who weaves her thin web
50 aloft spread her work over the neglected name of 10
Manlius. For how much sorrow of heart the wily
goddess of Amathus gave me, ye know, and in
what manner she has overthrown me. When I was
burning as hotly as the Trinacrian rock and the
Malian water at Oetean Thermopylae, when my sad
55 eyes never rested from wasting with perpetual tears, 15
nor my cheeks from streaming with a flood of
sorrow;—as in the top of a lofty mountain a bright
stream leaps forth from a moss-grown rock, and
gushing headlong down the steep valley crosses the
60 mid way thronged by the people, a sweet solace in 20
his labour to the weary wayfarer when sultry heat
makes the parched fields gape; and as to mariners

hic, velut in nigro iactatis turbine nautis
   lenius aspirans aura secunda venit
65 iam prece Pollucis, iam Castoris implorata,   25
   tale fuit nobis Allius auxilium.
is clausum lato patefecit limite campum,
   isque domum nobis isque dedit dominam,
ad quam communes exerceremus amores.
70   quo mea se molli candida diva pede   30
intulit et trito fulgentem in limine plantam
   innixa arguta constituit solea;
coniugis ut quondam flagrans advenit amore
   Protesilaeam Laudamia domum
75 inceptam frustra, nondum cum sanguine sacro   35
   hostia caelestis pacificasset eros.
nil mihi tam valde placeat, Rhamnusia virgo,
   quod temere invitis suscipiatur eris.
quam ieiuna pium desideret ara cruorem,
80   doctast amisso Laudamia viro,   40
coniugis ante coacta novi dimittere collum
   quam veniens una atque altera rursus hiemps
noctibus in longis avidum saturasset amorem,
   posset ut abrupto vivere coniugio,
85 quod scibant Parcae non longo tempore abesse, 45
   si miles muros isset ad Iliacos:
nam tum Helenae raptu primores Argivorum
   coeperat ad sese Troia ciere viros.
Troia (nefas) commune sepulcrum Asiae Europae-
      que,
90   Troia virum et virtutum omnium acerba cinis, 50
quaene etiam nostro letum miserabile fratri
   attulit. ei misero frater adempte mihi,
[ei misero fratri iucundum lumen ademptum,
   tecum una totast nostra sepulta domus;
95 omnia tecum una perierunt gaudia nostra,   55
   quae tuus in vita dulcis alebat amor].

tossed by the black storm comes a favouring breeze
with gentler breath, sought by prayer now to Pollux,
65 now to Castor;—such an aid to me was Manlius; he 25
opened a broad track across the fenced field, he gave
me access to a house and its mistress, under whose
roof we should together enjoy each his own love.
70 Thither my fair goddess delicately stepped, and set 30
the sole of her shining foot on the smooth threshold,
as she pressed on her slender sandal: even as once
Laodamia came burning with love to the house of
Protesilaus, that house begun in vain, since not yet
75 had a victim's sacred blood appeased the Lords of 35
heaven.   Lady of Rhamnus, never may that please
me which is undertaken amiss without the will of our
Lords.

How much the starved altar craves for the blood
80 of pious sacrifices, Laodamia learnt by the loss of 40
her husband; forced to loose her arms from the neck
of her new spouse, before the coming of one and
then a second winter should content her eager love
in the long nights, that she might endure to live,
85 though her marriage bond was broken off; and this 45
the Fates had ordained to come in no long time, if
once he went as a soldier to the walls of Ilium.

For then, because of Helen's rape, had Troy
begun to summon against herself the chieftains of
90 the Argives, Troy—O horror!—the common grave 50
of Europe and Asia, Troy the untimely tomb of all
heroes and heroic deeds: Troy brought pitiable death
to my brother also; ah me, my brother taken from
me unhappy, alas! dear light of my eyes, taken from
thy unhappy brother: with thee now is all my house
95 buried; all my joys have perished together with thee, 55
which while thou wert alive thy sweet love cherished.

16—2

quem nunc tam longe non inter nota sepulcra
   nec prope cognatos compositum cineres,
sed Troia obscena, Troia infelice sepultum
100   detinet extremo terra aliena solo.   60
ad quam tum properans fertur [simul] undique
       pubes
   Graeca penetralis deseruisse focos,
ne Paris abducta gavisus libera moecha
   otia pacato degeret in thalamo.
105 quo tibi tum casu, pulcherrima Laudamia,   65
   ereptumst vita dulcius atque anima
coniugium: tanto te absorbens vertice amoris
   aestus in abruptum detulerat barathrum,
quale ferunt Grai Pheneum prope Cylleneum
110   siccare emulsa pingue palude solum,   70
quod quondam caesis montis fodisse medullis
   audit falsiparens Amphitryoniades,
tempore quo certa Stymphalia monstra sagitta
   perculit imperio deterioris eri,
115 pluribus ut caeli tereretur ianua divis,   75
   Hebe nec longa virginitate foret.
sed tuus altus amor barathro fuit altior illo,
   qui tamen indomitam ferre iugum docuit:
nam nec tam carum confecto aetate parenti
120   una caput seri nata nepotis alit,   80
qui, cum divitiis vix tandem inventus avitis
   nomen testatas intulit in tabulas,
impia derisi gentilis gaudia tollens
   suscitat a cano vulturium capiti:
125 nec tantum niveo gavisast ulla columbo   85
   compar, quae multo dicitur improbius
oscula mordenti semper decerpere rostro,
   quam quae praecipue multivolast mulier.

Thee now far, far away, not among familiar graves, nor laid to rest near the ashes of thy kinsfolk, but buried in hateful Troy, ill-omened Troy, a foreign land holds in a distant soil.

To Troy at that time all the youth of Greece is said to have hastened together, deserting their hearths and homes, that Paris might not enjoy undisturbed leisure in a peaceful chamber, rejoicing in the rape of his paramour.

By that sad chance then, fairest Laodamia, wast thou bereft of thy husband sweeter to thee than life and soul; so strong the tide of love, so whelming the eddy that bore thee into the sheer abyss, deep as that gulf which (say the Greeks) near Cyllenian Pheneus drains away the swamp, and dries up the ground which erst the false-fathered son of Amphitryon is said to have dug out, cutting away the heart of the hill, what time with sure shaft he hit the monsters of Stymphalus at the bidding of a meaner lord, that the door of heaven might be frequented by more gods, and that Hebe might not long be unmated. But thy deep love was deeper than that gulf, which taught thee though untamed to bear the yoke.

Not so dear to her age-stricken parent is the head of the late-born grandchild which his only daughter nurses, who, scarce at length appearing as an heir to ancestral wealth, and having his name brought into the witnessed tablets, puts an end to the unnatural joy of the kinsman, now in his turn derided, and drives away the vulture that waits for the hoary head; nor did any dove so much delight in her snowy mate, who is said to be ever snatching kisses with biting beak, more wantonly than any woman, be she amorous beyond others' measure. You alone

sed tu horum magnos vicisti sola furores,
130   ut semel es flavo conciliata viro.   90
aut nihil aut paulo cui tum concedere digna
    lux mea se nostrum contulit in gremium,
quam circumcursans hinc illinc saepe Cupido
    fulgebat crocina candidus in tunica.
135 quae tamenetsi uno non est contenta Catullo,   95
    rara verecundae furta feremus erae,
ne nimium simus stultorum more molesti.
    saepe etiam Iuno, maxima caelicolum,
coniugis in culpa flagrantem concoquit iram,
140   noscens omnivoli plurima facta Iovis.   100
    †atque nec divis homines componier aequumst,

                    *   *   *   *

    ingratum tremuli tolle parentis onus.
nec tamen illa mihi dextra deducta paterna
    fragrantem Assyrio venit odore domum,
145 sed furtiva dedit *muta munuscula nocte,   105
    ipsius ex ipso dempta viri gremio.
quare illud satis est, si nobis is datur unis,
    quem lapide illa, dies, candidiore notat.
hoc tibi, quod potui, confectum carmine munus
150   pro multis, Alli, redditur officiis,   110
ne vestrum scabra tangat rubigine nomen
    haec atque illa dies atque alia atque alia.
huc addent divi quam plurima, quae Themis olim
    antiquis solitast munera ferre piis:
155 sitis felices et tu simul et tua vita   115
    et domus [illa], in qua lusimus, et domina,
et qui principio nobis †terram dedit aufert,†
    a quo sunt primo *mi omnia nata bona.
et longe ante omnes mihi quae me carior ipsost,
160   lux mea, qua viva vivere dulce mihist.   120

surpassed the desires of these, when once you were
130 matched with your golden-haired husband.   90

Not at all or but little worthy to yield to her was
my bright one who came into my bosom ; and often
around her flitting hither and thither Cupid shone
white in vest of saffron hue.   And though she is not
135 content with Catullus alone, I will bear the faults, for 95
few they are, of my modest mistress, lest we become
as tiresome as jealous fools.   Juno, too, greatest of
the heavenly ones, often keeps down her anger for
her husband's fault, as she learns the many amours
140 of all-fickle Jove.   Yet since it is not fit that men 100
should be compared with gods   *   *   *
away, then, with the hateful severity of an anxious
father.   And after all, she did not come for me led
by her father's hand into a house fragrant with
145 Assyrian odours, but gave me in the silent night 105
sweet stolen gifts, taken from the very bosom of her
husband himself.   Wherefore it is enough if to me
alone is given that day which she marks with a
whiter stone.

This gift—'twas all I could—set forth in poetry
150 is returned to you, Allius, for many kind offices ; 110
lest this and that day, and another and another
should touch your name with corroding rust.   To this
the gods will add those countless gifts which Themis
of old was wont to give to pious men of ancient
time.   May ye be happy, both you, and with you
155 your dear Life, and the house in which you and I 115
sported, and its mistress, and he who first [   ]
for us, from whom first all those good things had
their springing for me.   And far before all, she who
is dearer to me than myself, my Light, whose life
160 alone makes it sweet to me to live.   120

LXX

Nulli se dicit mulier mea nubere malle
  quam mihi, non si se Iuppiter ipse petat.
dicit: sed mulier cupido quod dicit amanti
  in vento et rapida scribere oportet aqua.

LXXII

Dicebas quondam solum te nosse Catullum,
  Lesbia, nec prae me velle tenere Iovem.
dilexi tum te non tantum ut vulgus amicam,
  sed pater ut gnatos diligit et generos.
nunc te cognovi: quare etsi impensius uror,   5
  multo mi tamen es vilior et levior.
qui potis est? inquis. quod amantem iniuria talis
  cogit amare magis, sed bene velle minus.

LXXIII

Desine de quoquam quicquam bene velle mereri
  aut aliquem fieri posse putare pium.
omnia sunt ingrata, nihil fecisse benigne
  *prodest, immo etiam taedet obestque magis:
ut mihi, quem nemo gravius nec acerbius urget,   5
  quam modo qui me unum atque unicum amicum
    habuit.

LXX

The woman I love says that there is no one whom she would rather marry than me, not if Jupiter himself were to woo her. Says;—but what a woman says to her ardent lover should be written in wind and running water.

LXXII

You used once to say that Catullus was your only friend, Lesbia, and that you would not have Jupiter rather than me. I loved you then, not only as the common sort loves a mistress, but as a father loves his sons and sons-in-law. Now I know you; 5 and therefore, though I burn more ardently, yet you are in my sight much less worthy and lighter. How can that be? you say. Because such an injury as this drives a lover to love more, but to like less.

LXXIII

Leave off wishing to deserve any thanks from anyone, or thinking that anyone can ever become grateful. All this wins no thanks; to have acted kindly does no good, rather it is a weariness and harmful; so is it now with me, who am vexed and 5 troubled by no one so bitterly as by him who but now held me for his one and only friend.

LXXV

Huc est mens deducta tua, mea Lesbia, culpa,
    atque ita se officio perdidit ipsa suo,
ut iam nec bene velle queat tibi, si optima fias,
    nec desistere amare, omnia si facias.

LXXVI

Siqua recordanti benefacta priora voluptas
    est homini, cum se cogitat esse pium,
nec sanctam violasse fidem, nec foedere in ullo
    divum ad fallendos numine abusum homines,
multa parata manent in longa aetate, Catulle,   5
    ex hoc ingrato gaudia amore tibi.
nam quaecumque homines bene cuiquam aut dicere
            possunt
    aut facere, haec a te dictaque factaque sunt;
omnia quae ingratae perierunt credita menti.
    quare cur te iam *a! amplius excrucies?   10
quin tu animum offirmas atque istinc teque reducis
    et dis invitis desinis esse miser?
difficilest longum subito deponere amorem.
    difficilest, verum hoc qualubet efficias.
una salus haec est, hoc est tibi pervincendum :   15
    hoc facias, sive id non pote sive pote.
o di, si vestrumst misereri, aut si quibus umquam
    extremam iam ipsa in morte tulistis opem,
me miserum aspicite et, si vitam puriter egi,
    eripite hanc pestem perniciemque mihi.   20

LXXV

To this point is my mind reduced by your fault, Lesbia, and has so ruined itself by its own devotion, that now it can neither wish you well though you should become the best of women, nor cease to love you though you do the worst that can be done.

LXXVI

If a man can take any pleasure in recalling the thought of kindnesses done, when he thinks that he has been a true friend; and that he has not broken sacred faith, nor in any compact has used the majesty of the gods in order to deceive men, there are many joys in a long life for you, Catullus, 5 earned from this thankless love. For whatever kindness man can show to man by word or deed has been said and done by you. All this was entrusted to an ungrateful heart, and is lost: why then should you torment yourself now any more? 10 Why do you not settle your mind firmly, and draw back, and cease to be miserable, in despite of the gods? It is difficult suddenly to lay aside a long-standing love. It is difficult; but you should accomplish it, one way or another. This is the only safety, this you must carry through, this you 15 are to do, whether it is possible or impossible. Ye gods, if mercy is your attribute, or if ye ever brought aid to any at the very moment of death, look upon me in my trouble, and if I have led a pure life, take away this plague and ruin from me. 20

heu, mihi surrepens imos ut torpor in artus
    expulit ex omni pectore laetitias!
non iam illud quaero, contra me ut diligat illa,
    aut, quod non potis est, esse pudica velit:
ipse valere opto et taetrum hunc deponere mor-
      bum.   25
    o di, reddite mi hoc pro pietate mea.

LXXVII

Rufe mihi frustra ac nequiquam credite amico
    (frustra? immo magno cum pretio atque malo),
sicine subrepsti mi, atque intestina perurens
    ei misero eripuisti omnia nostra bona?
eripuisti, heu heu nostrae crudele venenum   5
    vitae, heu heu nostrae pestis amicitiae.

LXXXI

Nemone in tanto potuit populo esse, Iuventi,
    bellus homo, quem tu diligere inciperes,
praeterquam iste tuus moribunda ab sede Pisauri
    hospes inaurata pallidior statua,
qui tibi nunc cordist, quem tu praeponere nobis   5
    audes, et nescis quod facinus facias?

LXXXII

Quinti, si tibi vis oculos debere Catullum
    aut aliud siquid carius est oculis,
eripere ei noli, multo quod carius illi
    est oculis seu quid carius est oculis.

Ah me! what a lethargy creeps into my inmost joints, and has cast out all joys from my heart! No longer is this my prayer, that she should love me in return, or, for that is impossible, that she should consent to be chaste. I would myself be well again and put 25 away this baleful sickness. O ye gods, grant me this in return for my piety.

LXXVII

Rufus, whom I, your friend, trusted in vain, and to no purpose—in vain? nay rather at a great and ruinous price—have you stolen into my heart and burning into my vitals torn away, alas, all my blessings? Torn away, alas, alas! you the cruel 5 poison of my life, alas, alas! you the deadly bane of my friendship.

LXXXI

Could there not, Juventius, be found in all this people a pretty fellow whom you might begin to like, besides that friend of yours from the sickly region of Pisaurum, paler than a gilded statue, who now is dear to you, whom you presume to prefer 5 to me, and know not what a deed you do?

LXXXII

Quinctius, if you wish Catullus to owe his eyes to you, or aught else that is dearer than eyes, if dearer aught there be, do not take from him what is much dearer to him than his eyes, or aught besides that dearer is than eyes.

LXXXIII

Lesbia mi praesente viro mala plurima dicit:
    haec illi fatuo maxima laetitiast.
mule, nihil sentis. si nostri oblita taceret,
    sana esset: nunc quod gannit et obloquitur,
non solum meminit, sed quae multo acrior est res, 5
    iratast. hoc est, uritur et loquitur.

LXXXIV

Chommoda dicebat, si quando commoda vellet
    dicere, et insidias Arrius hinsidias,
et tum mirifice sperabat se esse locutum,
    cum quantum poterat dixerat hinsidias.
credo, sic mater, sic Liber avunculus eius,   5
    sic maternus avus dixerat atque avia.
hoc misso in Syriam requierant omnibus aures:
    audibant eadem haec leniter et leviter,
nec sibi postilla metuebant talia verba,
    cum subito affertur nuntius horribilis,   10
Ionios fluctus, postquam illuc Arrius isset,
    iam non Ionios esse, sed Hionios.

LXXXV

Odi et amo. quare id faciam, fortasse requiris.
    nescio, sed fieri sentio et excrucior.

LXXXIII

Lesbia says many hard things to me in the presence of her husband, a great joy to the fool. You understand nothing, dull mule. If she forgot me and were silent, she would be heart-whole. But as it is, her snarling and railing means this: she not only remembers but—a much more serious thing— 5 she is angry; that is, she is burning all the while she is talking.

LXXXIV

Arrius if he wanted to say 'honours' used to say '*h*onours' and for 'ambush,' '*h*ambush'; and thought he had spoken marvellous well, whenever he said '*h*ambush' with as much emphasis as possible. So, no doubt, his mother had said, so Liber 5 his uncle, so his grandfather and grandmother on the mother's side. When he was sent into Syria, all our ears had a holiday; they heard the same syllables pronounced quietly and lightly, and had no fear of such words for the future: when on a sudden 10 a dreadful message arrives, that the Ionian waves, ever since Arrius went there, are henceforth not Ionian, but *H*ionian.

LXXXV

I hate and love. Why I do so, perhaps you ask. I know not, but I feel it, and I am in torment.

LXXXVI

Quintia formosast multis; mihi candida, longa,
    rectast. haec ego sic singula confiteor,
totum illud formosa nego: nam nulla venustas,
    nulla in tam magnost corpore mica salis.
Lesbia formosast, quae cum pulcherrima totast,   5
    tum omnibus una omnis surripuit Veneres.

LXXXVII

Nulla potest mulier tantum se dicere amatam
    vere, quantum a me Lesbia amata mea's.
nulla fides ullo fuit umquam foedere tanta,
    quanta in amore tuo ex parte reperta meast.

XCI

Non ideo, Gelli, sperabam te mihi fidum
    in misero hoc nostro, hoc perdito amore fore,
quod te cognossem bene constantemve putarem
    aut posse a turpi mentem inhibere probro,
sed neque quod matrem nec germanam esse vide-
        bam   5
    hanc tibi, cuius me magnus edebat amor.
et quamvis tecum multo coniungerer usu,
    non satis id causae credideram esse tibi.
tu satis id duxti: tantum tibi gaudium in omni
    culpast, in quacumque est aliquid sceleris.   10

LXXXVI

Quintia is thought beautiful by many; I think her fair, tall, well-grown. I so far allow each of these points, but I demur to 'beautiful': for she has no grace; there is not in the whole length of her tall person one mite of salt. Lesbia is 5 beautiful: for she possesses all the beauties, and has stolen the graces from all the women, all to herself.

LXXXVII

No woman can say truly that she is loved as much as you, Lesbia mine, are loved by me. No faithfulness in any bond was ever such as has been found on my side in my love for you.

XCI

I hoped, Gellius, that you would be true to me in this miserable, this ruinous love of mine, not on the ground that I knew you well, or thought that you were honourable or could restrain your mind from baseness or villainy, but because I saw that she, whose 5 mighty love was consuming me, was neither mother nor sister of yours. And although I was connected with you by much familiar friendship, I had not thought that *that* was reason enough for you. You thought it enough: so much delight do you take in any vice in which there is something of dis- 10 honour.

XCII

Lesbia mi dicit semper male nec tacet umquam
  de me: Lesbia me dispeream nisi amat.
quo signo? quia sunt totidem mea: deprecor illam
  assidue, verum dispeream nisi amo.

XCIII

Nil nimium studeo, Caesar, tibi velle placere,
  nec scire utrum sis albus an ater homo.

XCV

Zmyrna mei Cinnae, nonam post denique messem
  quam coeptast nonamque edita post hiemem,
milia cum interea quingenta † Hortensius uno
  *   *   *   *
Zmyrna cavas Satrachi penitus mittetur ad undas, 5
  Zmyrnam cana diu saecula pervoluent.
at Volusi annales Paduam morientur ad ipsam
  et laxas scombris saepe dabunt tunicas.
parva mei mihi sint cordi monumenta [sodalis],
  at populus tumido gaudeat Antimacho.   10

XCVI

Si quicquam mutis gratum acceptumve sepulcris
  accidere a nostro, Calve, dolore potest,
quo desiderio veteres renovamus amores
  atque olim amissas flemus amicitias,
certe non tanto mors immatura dolorist   5
  Quintiliae, quantum gaudet amore tuo.

XCII

Lesbia always speaks ill of me, and is always talking of me. May I perish if Lesbia does not love me. By what token? because it is just the same with me. I am perpetually crying out upon her, but may I perish if I do not love her.

XCIII

I have no very great desire to make myself agreeable to you, Caesar, nor to know whether your complexion is light or dark.

XCV

My friend Cinna's *Smyrna*, published at last nine harvest-tides and nine winters after it was begun, whilst Hortensius [has brought out] five hundred thousand [verses] in one [year]

* * * *

Smyrna will travel as far away as the deep-channeled streams of Satrachus. But the Annals of Volusius will die by the river Padua where they were born, and will often furnish a loose wrapper for mackerels. Let the modest memorials of my friend be dear to me, and let the vulgar rejoice in their windy Antimachus.

XCVI

If the silent grave can receive any pleasure, or sweetness at all from our grief, Calvus, the grief and regret with which we renew our old loves, and weep for long lost friendships, surely Quintilia feels less sorrow for her too early death, than pleasure from your love.

XCIX

Surripui tibi dum ludis, mellite Iuventi,
   saviolum dulci dulcius ambrosia.
verum id non impune tuli : namque amplius horam
   suffixum in summa me memini esse cruce,
dum tibi me purgo nec possum fletibus ullis   5
   tantillum vestrae demere saevitiae.
      .   .   .   .

praeterea infesto miserum me tradere Amori
   non cessasti omnique excruciare modo,
ut mi ex ambrosia mutatum iam foret illud
   saviolum tristi tristius helleboro.
quam quoniam poenam misero proponis amori   15
   numquam iam posthac basia surripiam.

CI

Multas per gentes et multa per aequora vectus
   advenio has miseras, frater, ad inferias,
ut te postremo donarem munere mortis
   et mutam nequiquam alloquerer cinerem,
quandoquidem fortuna mihi tete abstulit ipsum,   5
   heu miser indigne frater adempte mihi.
nunc tamen interea haec, prisco quae more pa-
       rentum
   tradita sunt tristi munere ad inferias,
accipe fraterno multum manantia fletu,
   atque in perpetuum, frater, ave atque vale.   10

XCIX

I stole a kiss from you, honey-sweet Juventius,
while you were playing, a kiss sweeter than sweet
ambrosia. But not unpunished; for I remember
how for more than an hour I hung impaled on the
top of the gallows tree, while I was excusing myself 5
to you, yet could not with all my tears take away
ever so little from your anger . . . . Besides,
you made haste to deliver your unhappy lover to 11
angry Love, and to torture him in every manner, so
that that kiss, changed from ambrosia, was now
more bitter than bitter hellebore. Since then you 15
impose this penalty on my unlucky love, henceforth
I will never steal any kisses.

CI

Wandering through many countries and over
many seas I come, my brother, to these sorrowful
obsequies, to present you with the last guerdon of
death, and speak, though in vain, to your silent
ashes, since fortune has taken your own self away 5
from me—alas, my brother, so cruelly torn from
me! Yet now meanwhile take these offerings,
which by the custom of our fathers have been
handed down—a sorrowful tribute—for a funeral
sacrifice; take them, wet with many tears of
a brother, and for ever, my brother, hail and 10
farewell!

CII

Si quicquam tacite commissumst fido †ab amico,
  cuius sit penitus nota fides animi,
meque esse invenies illorum iure sacratum,
  Corneli, et factum me esse puta Harpocratem.

CIII

Aut, sodes, mihi redde decem sestertia, Silo,
  deinde esto quamvis saevus et indomitus:
aut, si te nummi delectant, desine quaeso
  leno esse atque idem saevus et indomitus.

CIV

Credis me potuisse meae maledicere vitae,
  ambobus mihi quae carior est oculis?
non potui, nec si possem tam perdite amarem:
  sed tu cum Tappone omnia monstra facis.

CV

Mentula conatur Pipleum scandere montem:
  Musae furcillis praecipitem eiciunt.

CII

If ever any secret whatsoever was entrusted in confidence by a faithful friend, the loyalty of whose heart was fully known, you will find both that I am consecrated by their rite, Cornelius, and you may think that I am become a very Harpocrates.

CIII

Prithee, Silo, either give me back the ten sestertia, and then you may be as violent and overbearing as you like; or, if the money gives you pleasure, don't try, I beg, to ply your trade and be at the same time violent and overbearing.

CIV

Do you think that I ever could have spoken ill of my life, her who is dearer to me than both my eyes? I could never have done it; nor, if I could help it, would I be so ruinously in love. But you and Tappo make out everything to be prodigious.

CV

Mentula strives to climb the Piplean mount: the Muses with pitchforks drive him out headlong.

CVII

Sicui quid cupido optantique optigit umquam
　　insperanti, hoc est gratum animo proprie.
quare hoc est gratum nobis quoque, carius auro,
　　quod te restituis, Lesbia, mi cupido,
restituis cupido atque insperanti, ipsa refers te　　5
　　nobis: o lucem candidiore nota!
quis me uno vivit felicior, aut magis hac rem
　　optandam in vita dicere quis poterit?

CVIII

Si, Comini, populi arbitrio tua cana senectus
　　spurcata impuris moribus intereat,
non equidem dubito quin primum inimica bonorum
　　lingua exsecta avido sit data volturio,
effossos oculos voret atro gutture corvus,　　5
　　intestina canes, cetera membra lupi.

CIX

Iucundum, mea vita, mihi proponis amorem
　　hunc nostrum inter nos perpetuumque fore.
di magni, facite ut vere promittere possit,
　　atque id sincere dicat et ex animo,
ut liceat nobis tota perducere vita　　5
　　aeternum hoc sanctae foedus amicitiae.

CVII

If anything ever happened to any one who eagerly longed and never hoped, that is a true pleasure to the mind. And so to me too this is a pleasure more precious than gold, that you, Lesbia, restore yourself to me who longed for you, restore to 5 me who longed, but never hoped, yes, you yourself give yourself back to me. O happy day, blessed with the whiter mark! What living wight is more lucky than I; or who can say that any fortune in life is more desirable than this?

CVIII

If, Cominius, your gray old age, soiled as it is by an impure life, should be brought to an end by the choice of the people, I for my part do not doubt that first of all your tongue, the enemy of good citizens, would be cut out and quickly given to the greedy vulture, your eyes torn out and swallowed 5 down the raven's black throat, while the dogs would devour your bowels, the rest of your members the wolves.

CIX

You promise to me, my life, that this love of ours shall be pleasant and last for ever between us. Ye great gods, grant that she may be able to keep this promise truly, and that she may say it sincerely and from her heart, so that we may be allowed to 5 extend through all our life this eternal compact of hallowed friendship.

CXIV

Firmano saltu non falso Mentula dives
    fertur, qui tot res in se habet egregias,
aucupia omne genus, piscis, prata, arva ferasque.
    nequiquam : fructus sumptibus exsuperat.
quare concedo sit dives, dum omnia desint.   5
    saltus laudemus commoda, dum ipse egeat.

CXV

Mentula habet †instar triginta iugera prati,
    quadraginta arvi : cetera sunt maria.
cur non divitiis Croesum superare potis sit
    uno qui in saltu †totmoda possideat,
prata, arva, ingentis silvas †saltusque paludesque   5
    usque ad Hyperboreos et mare ad Oceanum?

        .   .   .   .

CXVI

Saepe tibi studioso animo venante requirens
    carmina uti possem mittere Battiadae,
qui te lenirem nobis, neu conarere
    tela infesta *mihi mittere in usque caput,
hunc video mihi nunc frustra sumptum esse la-
      borem,   5
    Gelli, nec nostras hic valuisse preces.
contra nos tela ista tua evitamus amictu :
    at fixus nostris tu dabi' supplicium.

CXIV

Mentula is truly said to be rich in the possession of the grant of land at Firmum, which has so many fine things in it, fowling of all sorts, fish, meadow-land, corn-land, and game. All to no purpose; he outruns the produce of it by his expenses. So 5 I grant that he is rich, if you will allow that he lacks everything. Let us admire the advantages of his estate, so long as he himself is in want.

CXV

Mentula has something like thirty acres of grazing land, forty of plough land: the rest is salt water. How can he fail to surpass Croesus in wealth, who occupies so many good things in one estate, pasture, arable, vast woods and cattle-ranges and lakes as far as 5 the Hyperboreans and the Great Sea?

. . . .

CXVI

I have often cast about with busy questing mind how I could send to you some poems of Callimachus with which I might make you placable to me, and that you might not strive to send a shower of missiles to reach my head; but now I see that this labour 5 has been taken by me in vain, Gellius, and that my prayers have here availed nothing. Now in return I will parry those missiles of yours by wrapping my cloak round my arm; but you shall be pierced by mine and punished.

FRAGMENTA.

1. At non effugies meos iambos.

2. Hunc lucum tibi dedico consecroque Priape,
   qua domus tua Lampsacist quaque [silva], Priape,
   nam te praecipue in suis urbibus colit ora
   Hellespontia ceteris ostreosior oris.

3. $- \smile - \smile \smile$ de meo ligurrire libidost.

4. [$\smile - \smile -$ et Lario imminens Comum.]

5. Lucida qua splende[n]t [summi] carchesia mali.

FRAGMENTS.

1. But you shall not escape my iambics.

2. This inclosure I dedicate and consecrate to thee, O Priapus, at Lampsacus, where is thy house and sacred grove, O Priapus. For thee specially in its cities the Hellespontian coast worships, more abundant in oysters than all other coasts.

3. It is my fancy to taste on my own account.

4. And Comum built on the shore of lake Larius.

5. With which shines the top of the mast.

NOTES.

I 9, 10. Or (*qualecumque quidem patroni ut ergo* M.) 'whatever it is worth indeed; that for the merits of its (my) patron,' &c.

II 7. Or (*et solaciolum sui doloris, credo, et quo gravis acquiescat ardor* P. *cum—acquiescet* codd.) 'both as a solace to her pain, ah yes! and that her grievous smart may be lulled by it.' *quo* abl.

IV 18. *inde*, or 'thereafter.'

23. Or 'for her.'

24. Or (*novissime* M. and codd.) 'when last she came from the sea,' &c.

VI 1. Or 'your loves' = *amores* E.

VII 2. Either 'kissings of you' or 'kisses from you' = *a te datae*, and accordingly in 9.

VIII 14, 15. Or (*cum rogaberis nulla. Scelesta, vae te!* P.) 'when you are asked no more. Ah, poor wretch!' Perhaps *nullam noctem*.

IX 1. Or (*o meis a.*) 'preferred by me to all my friends, the whole three hundred thousand of them'; or (abl.), 'by three hundred thousand'; or perhaps, 'by three hundred miles.'

7. *facta*, or 'what you did there' = *tua facta*.

10. Or *quantumst—beatiorum* may = vocative, as III 2.

x. 8. Or 'seas,' but see Ellis's note.

10. Or (*nec*) 'neither the people themselves nor the praetors nor their staff.' *hoc praetore fuisse* is a possible emendation.

23. Or (*mi anime*) 'my dear.'

26. *Sarapim* G, *Serapini* O, *Serapim* R.M.

32. The reading is doubtful. *pararim* is ungrammatical; *paratis* (= *si parassem*) harsh.

XI 11. Or (*horribilem salum ult. Brit.* M) 'the dangerous sea and distant Britons.' This reading is supported by R. *horribiles ult.*; *horribilē salū ult.* would easily become *horribiles ult.*

XII 9. *disertus leporum* is classed by Roby, L. Gr. (1320) and Madvig (290 g) with *ingens virium, aevi maturus, vetus militiae*, 'in respect of': there is no need for emendation.

14. *exhibere* codd. If *ex Hibere* is read it will be 'from the Ebro country.'

XIV 14. Or (*continuo* adj.) 'the very next day'; as Ov. Fast. V 734, VI 720. Or 'on that very day.'

XVII 15, 16. Or *et* might be taken as = *sed*, 'now a maiden...ought to be guarded,' &c. *et—uvis* being parenthetical.

20. Or 'she' (*nulla*).

XXII 5. *palimpsesto* codd., 'can hardly be Latin' M.; but *referre in palimpseston, tabulas*, &c., the usual term, does not necessarily exclude *in palimpsesto relata*, the finished act. Cf. XXVIII 6—8. Perhaps *in palimpsestos* B.P.

11. *abhorret = absurdus est* M., 'unlike himself' E.

13. *tristius* of codd. is corrupt. I have translated *tritius*. Other emendations (none satisfactory) are *tersius* [*tertius*], *scitius*.

XXV 5. *locus desperatus*. The emendations proposed are no more than ingenious guesses. What is wanted is not a new idea (as *munerarios, vicarios, balnearios*), but something to carry out the idea of a storm at sea. Mr Mowat (*J. of Philol.* XIV 252) suggests *cum diva mater (Tethys) horias ostendit aestuantes*. I suspect that *trabes* (cf. IV 3), is hidden in *aries* and that *oscitantes* means 'gaping.'

XXVII 4. See M. *ebriose* of codd. may be for *ebriosae*,

'drunken Postumia, more drunken,' &c. : but in these MSS. *e* and *o* are interchangeable.

XXIX 9.   No satisfactory emendation is proposed.

21.   Of the many emendations of this verse two may be mentioned : (1) *timentque* [*ne*] *Galliae hunc, timent Britanniae* (Avant.) ; (2) *et huicne Gallia et metet Britannia* M.

24.   Another *locus desperatus*, not much mended by *urbis o pudet meae* E., *urbis ob luem ipsimae* M. (*ipsimae = dominae*, i.e. Rome), 'plague-sore of the mistress-town.' *urbis* (or *orbis*) *o piissimi*, 'most affectionate pair' Hpt. P. al.

XXX 4.   Or (*nec = non*) 'the deeds of deceivers please not at all,' &c. (see M. p. 114).

5.   *que* codd.   vv. ll. *quod quos quem.*   M. reads *quom*, and puts a comma after *malis*, 'since you neglect me &c., what are men to do?'

7.   *me* may be taken either with *iubebas* or with *inducens.*

XXXI 10.   *lecto* abl.   Cf. II 7 note.

13.   *Lydiae* codd., 'Lydian,' i.e. Etruscan ; al. *limpidae liquidae.*   H.V.M. (with Calverley) suggests that *Lydiae* may mean 'golden,' i.e. from Pactolus.

14.   Or (taking *ridete* with *cachinni* voc., as III 1, 2 *quantumst* ; *quicquid est domi cachinnorum = omnes cachinni*), 'laugh out, all the laughter there is in my home.'   Cf. IX 10.

XXXIV 23.   Or (*Ancique* Scal.), 'and of Ancus.'   See E.'s note.

XXXVI 9, 10.   Or (*et haec pessima sic puella vidit* | *ioco se lepido v. d.* P.), 'and the lady saw that these were the "worst writings" that she was thus devoting to the gods in merry jest' —or *pessima* may go with *puella*, as LV 10.   *vidit* is probably corrupt.

By *pessimus poeta* Lesbia meant Catullus ; Catullus, Volusius. Cf. Hor. Carm. I xvi 2.

XXXVIII 6.   Either (1) 'is it thus you treat my friend?' (perhaps alluding to some quarrel with Juventius), or (2) 'my tale of love' E. ; in any case not *= amorem.*

8.   *lacrimis*, θρῆνοι.

XXXIX 11. *parcus* codd. (*pinguis* gloss. Vat.); al. *pastus fartus*; *porcus* Scal. P., 'an Umbrian pig.' Cf. Pers. III 74 *pinguibus Umbris.*

XLI 1. Or (*anne sana* B.) 'is she in her right mind?' cf. 7.

XLII 16. Or (*pote, ut ruborem…ore, conclamate* &c. M.), 'if nothing else can do so, in order to extort a blush from her brazen face, bawl out,' &c. This reading carries the sense on, and avoids the 'awkward stop' at the end of 17; but has no MS. authority.

XLIV 12. *legi* codd., 21 *legit* codd. Two explanations of this poem are given, according as *legi* or *legit* is read in 12, 21.

(1) (*legi*) Catullus, invited to dine with Sestius, read one of his speeches, caught cold from it, and did not go to dinner;

(2) (*legit*) Catullus was invited to dine with Sestius; went there, heard him read, and came away with a chill.

(2) makes better sense, reading *fecit* (B.) for *legit*.

21. *tunc—cum*, 'just when I have read,' of a single occasion, or 'only when I happen to read.' *cum* almost = *quoties*.

XLV 8. *ut ante* of codd. has probably come in from 17. I follow Dr Postgate's reading. This makes three sneezes: (1) *dextra* 9, (2) *sinistra* 8 and *sinistram* 17, (3) *dextram* 18; the first from the right, the second from the left, the third from the right again. (*Journal of Philology* XVII 237 sqq.) Dr Verrall suggests (*ibid.* 239 n.) that there were two pairs of sneezes; right and left at 8, 9, left and right at 17, 18. For Munro's view see his *Criticisms*, 120 sqq.

16. Or 'than to you,' understanding *quam tibi*: but *sic* (the formula of a vow) implies *magis magisque*, corresponding to *maior acriorque*, and this is simpler and more natural.

XLVII 2. *fames munda* (for *mundi* codd.) = *fames mera* Mart. III lviii 45.

XLIX 7. *omniums* is the reading of R.

L 2. Or (*invicem*) 'in turns.'

LI a 11. Or (*geminae*) 'both my ears…my eyes are

quenched in night.' *gemina* has MS. authority, *geminae* is more in Catullus's manner. Cf. LXIII 75.

LV 9. Corrupt. *avelli sinite* Avant., *avellent…puellae?* E. '*avertistis, saepe fl.*' are proposed as emendations.

22. *vostri sis, nostri sis* codd. *nostri sis* E. would mean 'so long as I can get to you and tell you my secrets.'

23—32 appear in the MSS. as a separate poem. They are usually inserted, as here, after 13. But they come in awkwardly wherever they are placed; and the poem cannot be reconstructed with any certainty, and is probably imperfect.

LVII 7. *lecticulo* O, *lectulo* cett. codd. See M. p. 131. If *mane* (X 27), altered *metri gr.* into *mane me*, is the right reading, so here O may have altered *lectulo* into *lecticulo*. At any rate the emendation is not necessary.

LVIII 5. Or (*magnanimis*) 'the high-minded descendants.'

LXI 77. Or (*ades*) 'bride, come forth,' or (*claustra pandite ianuae, virgines*) 'throw back the bars of the door, ye maidens,' cf. 227 *claudite ostia, virgines*.

79. *tardet* prob. from *tardeo* v.n. The codd. are defective here and at 110, and no complete sense can be made out.

96. *viderit* = *visura sit*, translating Callimachus' ὄψεται ἠώς.

167. Or (*unus* codd.) 'one special guest' (E.), at the *cena nuptialis.*

200. Or (*cupis cupis*) 'desire what you desire.' *capis* of almost all codd. is, if not the original reading, a very early correction.

219. *inscieis…omnibus* codd. Catullus is not likely to have left one open short syllable (*omnibŭs*) in a poem in which synaphea is strictly observed. *omnibus…insciis, omnibus…obviis,* are proposed by Edd.

LXII 1. Or 'in heaven.'

11, 32. *aequalis* is read by all codd. 11, by T only 32.

17. Or (*convertite,* T.) 'turn your minds hither.'

35. Or (*eosdem* codd.) 'you overtake unchanged.'

40. Or (*contusus conclusus* codd.) 'bruised.' *convolsus* T, cf. LXIV 40.

45, 56. Or 'whilst—whilst.' The rendering given in the text is from Quintilian, IX 3, 16.

LXIII 5. Or (*devolvit ile acuto sibi pondere silicis*) 'cast down from him his members with the weight of the sharp flintstone,' or (*devolsit*, Hpt. B.) 'tore off'; the MSS. are corrupt.

9. Or (*typanum ac typum* M.) 'timbrel and medallion' (see M.'s note).

14. Or (*velut ex.*) 'as exiles.'

16. Or *pelagi*, codd. pler. *pelage* is accepted by Bentley, Lambinus and several editors.

18. Or (*ero*) 'at your master's bidding.'

31. Or (*animi* [*animo*] *egens*) 'reft of sense,' or (*animae egens*) 'breathless.'

39. Or 'the golden-faced sun' = χρυσοφαής.

43. Or (*trepidantem* R.) 'hurrying on his way,' or 'fluttering.'

45. *ipsa* R. edd. *ipse* cett. codd.

54. *omnia adirem* codd., or (*opaca, operta*) 'their hidden lurking-dens.'

58. Or (*remota*, acc. plur. neut.) 'be borne into these distant forests.'

63. Or (*ego enim vir* P., perhaps *eram*) 'for I was a man.'

84. *religat*, a very rare usage, but required by the sense. Cf. 76 and LXIV 174.

LXIV 14. Or (*freti*) 'the Nereids raised their faces from the foaming tide of the sea.'

23, 23a. For this reading see M. p. 147.

39. Or 'the trailing vine.'

65. Or (*luctantis*) 'straining,' or (*lucentis*) 'shining.'

100. *quanto* for *quantum* with *magis* by false analogy. *quam tum*, edd.

104. Or (*suscepit*) 'undertook,' or (*suspendit*) 'faltered' or 'dedicated' (cf. Verg. Geor. II 389. Aen. XII 766; Hor. Carm. I v 15).

109. So P. for *lateque cum eis...obvia* (*omnia*) of codd. ;

other emendations are *lateque et cominus* Avant.; *lateque comeis obit omnia* M.

119. *lamentatast, laetabatur, luctabatur*, are proposed.

140. Or (*misera*) 'these miseries.'

174. If *in Creta* is read, *religasset* would be 'moored,' 'made fast.' See note on 84.

178. *Idomeneos*, prob. = 'Cretan.' *Dia* is Naxos, but the emendation is conjectural; the codd. have *Ydoneos, idoneos, idmoneos*.

200, 201. *mente*, as often in Catullus, is little more than an adverbial sign.

205. Or (*quo motu* = cuius motu) 'at his gesture.'

213. Or (*castae*) 'as she left the walls of the virgin goddess.'

227. Or (*decet*) 'as the sail, &c., befits our grief.'

254. If *quae tum* is read, we must suppose a lacuna after 253 : if *qui tum* (of codd.), a lacuna after 255, unless we read *horum* 256, with Lachmann : if *quicum* (B.), *bacchantes* must be taken as = βάκχαι. 254, 255 are more appropriate to Bacchanalians than to Satyrs and Sileni.

270. *proclivas* or 'into ridges.'

283. Or (*parit*) 'brings to birth,' 'creates.'

287. Or (*doctis*) 'learned.' Other emendations are *claris* (Ital.), *crebris* (Lach.).

Minosim is corrupt. Other readings are *Haemonisin* (P.), *Magnesson* (E.), *Naiasin, Meliasin.*

296. *silici* may be abl., or (*Scythica*) 'with Scythian chain.'

309. Or (*annoso niveae*) 'snow-white bands rested on their aged heads'; codd. have *at roseo niveae.*

320. *Haec* = hae.

330. The codd. have *quae tibi flexo animo mentis perfundat amorem.* I print Muretus' emendation, which is accepted by almost all editors.

362. *morti*, not = *cadaveri*, but Polyxena is spoken of as a victim due for the death of Achilles, i. e. to the dead Achilles.

374. *iamdudum* may be construed with *cupido*, 'long-expecting.'

382. Codd. have *Pelei*, which can hardly be dative (cf. 336). If *Pelei* is read, it must be taken with *felicia carmina* 'a song of Peleus' happiness.' Perhaps *carmina* is corrupt, and some such word as *tempora* should be substituted. But the simplest emendation is *Peleo*.

404. Or (*penates*) 'the gods of the household.'

LXV 12.   Or (*tegam*) 'keep close or veiled in silence' E.

LXVI 15.   Or (*maritum*) 'of their husbands' P. *parumper, paventes, an quod aventum* are proposed.

19. *missum* or 'thrown' as Verg. Ecl. III 64 *malo me Galatea petit.*

28. Or (*quod non fortior ausit alis* codd. omn.) 'which none else could venture and so win the title of braver' E.

45. Codd. *propere*, al. *pepulere, rupere.*

77. Or (*expersa*) 'sprinkled with,' or *explens unguentis se,* 'delighting herself with.'

91. *sanguinis* codd., *unguinis*, Bentl.

93. *cur iterent* codd.   *corruerint* is commonly read since Lach.

non vestris (*ūris*) codd.   *vestris* prob. = *si*ᵛᵉ *ris*, written *ve siris, vestris.*

94. *fulgoret* (or *fulgeret*) = *fulguret.*   Codd. have *fulgeret*, but in these MSS. *e* and *o* are convertible.

LXVII 5.   Or (*voto servisse maligno*) 'lent yourself to the service of an ill-affected vow' (whether 'of its new mistress' (E.), or 'the old man's dying wish' (M.)) or (*voto servisse maligne*), 'to have carried out scurvily his wish and prayer' (M.).

12. Corrupt—*verum*—*is mos populi*; *verum istud populi fabula*; *verum est vox populi*, &c. have been conjectured.

37—40 may be given either to Catullus or to the House-door.

LXVIII a 12.   Or (*torruerit*) 'burnt me up,' or *in me quo corruerit genere*, 'how she has rushed down npon me'; cf. Hor. Carm. I xix 9.

32. *arguta* or 'creaking.'

44. Or taking *abrupto* as = *abrepto* (M.) 'though her husband was torn from her' (*abrupto sidere* Verg. Æn. XII 451 might thus mean 'when the sun is hidden').

51. *que vetet id* codd., *quaene etiam* (Heins.) is commonly read. Other conjectures are *quae taetre id* (M.), *qualiter id* (*et ?*) (E.), *quae vel idem* (M.R.)

53. Or 'ah, pleasing light of life taken from my miserable brother!'

100. Or *furta* as 96.

101. *at quia* for *atque* of codd. *atqui* is also read.

102. Or 'take up the weary burden of the decrepit father'; with allusion to a supposed episode of Aeneas and Anchises in the lost verses.

105. Or (*mira*) 'wondrous.'

117. Nothing satisfactory can be made out of *terram dedit aufert* of codd. M. translates *terram* 'firm ground.' Under *aufert* some name (*Anser, Ufens, Afer*) may be concealed.

LXXII 8. 'Kindles perforce the more, but grows less kind' (H.V.M.) or 'to love her more, but less to wish her well.'

LXXIII 3, 4. P. punctuates *omnia sunt ingrata, nihil fecisse benigne; immo taedet obestque et* (*ei ?*) *magis atque magis*, for *immo etiam tedet obestque magisque magis* of codd. Other emendations of 4 are *prodest, iam iuvat, iuverit.*

LXXVII 6. Or (*pectus*) 'the trusted breast on which my friendship leaned' (E.).

LXXXIII 6. 'The heart flames, the mouth proclaims' (H.V.M.), or (*coquitur*) 'she is burning and glowing.' *hoc est* commonly introduces a proverb.

LXXXIV 5. Or (*liber*) 'the freeman,' i.e. the first of the line who was freeborn.

XCI 3. Or (*non nossem* Avant.), 'it was not that I did not know you [as I did].' *cognossem*, 'supposed but false reason' (E.). *cognossem* would imply known probity.

XCV 3. *Hortensius* is corrupt. M. supplies the lacuna by *Hatrianus in uno | versiculorum anno putidus evomuit.*

9. Or (*Phalaeci*) 'of my own Phalaecus' (M.).

XCVI 3. Or (*quom* M. and P.) 'when in sorrow,' &c.

CII 1. M. reads *tacite* for codd. *tacito*. P. *si quoi quid tacito commissumst fido et amico*, 'a silent and trusty friend.'

3. Or (comma after *illorum*) 'one of them, duly consecrate' (M.).

meque or 'that I too.' Cf. M. ad loc.

CVII 3. Or (*carior auro*), referring to Lesbia (P.).

CXIV 6. The reading of the MSS. *saltum laudemus dum modo ipse egeat* is probably corrupt. M. accepts it, taking *modo* as abl.: 'so long as he himself has no standard of moderation,' with a reference to CXV 5, 6. The reading in the text is Dr Postgate's (*Journal of Philology*, XXII 261).

CXV 1. Or (*iuxta*) Scal. 'nearly,' or (*vester* P.) 'your (Caesar's) friend.'

2. Or (*nemoris* M.) 'woodland.'

4. *tot bona* (P.), or *tot qui in saltu uno commoda*' (M.), for the corrupt *tot moda totmoda* of codd.

5. *saltus* is probably corrupt.

CXVI 1. Or (*studiose*) 'studiously searching,' or *studioso* may be taken as dative, 'at your desire.'

4. So P. reads for *telis infesta mitteremus que* of codd.

For EU product safety concerns, contact us at Calle de José Abascal, 56–1°,
28003 Madrid, Spain or eugpsr@cambridge.org.

www.ingramcontent.com/pod-product-compliance
Ingram Content Group UK Ltd.
Pitfield, Milton Keynes, MK11 3LW, UK
UKHW030905150625
459647UK00025B/2875